Death Goes to School

"The problem and solution of modern education"

Proverbs 9:10

Glennon Culwell

xulon PRESS

Table of Contents

Death Goes to School

Foreword

Glennon Culwell is a pastor of more than 40 years. I came to know Glennon and the truly remarkable man he is through his ministry to me personally during my college years and through my extended family who sat under his teaching for many years at the Scotts Valley Church that he pastored for almost 28 years. He is a devoted husband and loving father of five. In Death Goes to School, Pastor Culwell identifies destructive anti-family, anti-Christian and anti-child values widespread in our world and our culture.

As a parent and Christian university president I have watched as society has embraced our children and young adults with a growing list of damaging and sinful beliefs. Death Goes to School is a straightforward, biblical examination of these harmful assumptions and what Christ centered parents and Christian educators need to know to respond in truth and love. Pastor Culwell brings clear scriptural teaching to questions all parents face in "training up their children."

As parents follow well-established biblical principles, as outlined by the author of this book, parenting will result in great joy as my wife Gail and I can attest. Nothing has given us greater joy than sharing in the growth and maturating process of our three children – physically, mentally and spiritually.

Consequently, I would encourage the reader not to lose sight of this potential joy, seeing only what could be construed as trying, difficult responsibilities. As Dr. Bruce Clatterbuck, Executive Director of Next Generation Churches of Northern California and Nevada, observed upon reviewing the manuscript for this book, "…sometimes young families, fathers and mothers, reading books on how to rear their children, are so concerned with doing it right (which they should be), they miss the fun of enjoying their children." He further emphasized the importance of "balancing the responsibility and joy" in the parenting process.

Our great Father God created the first man and woman, the parents of the human race, and then joy of joys, He ordained that man and woman join Him in this blessed task of bringing new life into the world, commissioning them to "Be fruitful and multiply, fill the earth and subdue it."(Genesis 1:28) Thus began this most fulfilling experience, bringing new life into the world and sharing in the growth of that life to maturity.

Just contemplate the joy of parenting as young lives grow, form and mature into something beautiful and unique – lives with unlimited potential designed for eternity. We create products and materials from the work of our hands: building a house, sewing a garment, running a race, winning a game, cooking a meal, planting a garden, growing flowers, a thousand different things that produce great pleasure and a sense of satisfaction and fulfillment. Yet how much greater is the joy resulting from helping direct and form the lives of our children!

Give attention to these words from God as quoted by our author in this book,

"Behold, children are a heritage
from the Lord,
The fruit of the womb is a
a reward.
Like arrows in the hands of a
warrior,
So are the children of one's
youth.
Happy is the man who has his
quiver full of them..."(Psalm 127:3-5)

Yes, *"happy* is the man [and woman] who have "a quiver full" of children, and follow God's plan in rearing them.

Keep this promise of joy ever before you as you consider the problems that face our families and our youth, including the solution that will result when parental responsibilities are properly fulfilled, as outlined in this book, and the task will ever be seen as a delight in the face of the finished product!

I have found that in this post 9/11 World there is a resurgence of hopeful people looking for God's purpose and plan to be available for their lives. If you are one of those looking for clarity, wisdom, biblical teaching and loving admonition in rearing your children please read Death Goes to School.

Jon R. Wallace, DBA
President, Azusa Pacific University

Preface

Concern for our public educational system is expressed with alarm at every level of American society and government, from local school boards, teachers and administrators, through State and local government, the halls of congress, including action proposed by the President of the United States. Every right thinking person recognizes that there is a serious deficiency in our public school system, in spite of the presence of many dedicated teachers and administrators. The author of this book clearly establishes the validity of this statement through his carefully documented evidence, while referring to such incidents as that experienced at the Columbine High School. He accurately indicates that the major problem rests with the exclusion of God and values in the halls of public education.

Furthermore, one would agree that the plethora of solutions being suggested: increasing more and more finances, adjusting class sizes, more training for teachers, which may be needed in some cases, are not the solutions to a value deficient educational system.

In addition, it is obvious that many parents have abdicated their God-given responsibility for the teaching and training of their children, turning them over to institutions where God is excluded and the teaching of values is ignored or excluded, all in a "feel-good" sort of approach to life in which the student is encouraged, "if it feels good, do it!"

The author makes a compelling case that there have been movements, efforts, and pressures in our society designed to tear apart the fabric of God's design for the family. *Consequently, any genuine and lasting solution must include the involvement and oversight of parents in a traditional family setting.*

The author is to be commended regarding his thorough biblical approach in exploring parental and familial responsibilities. Particularly significant is the emphasis on the need for parents to study their children so as to know their God-given bent or design in order to develop God's design for their lives.

Consequently, loving discipline will be essential, an ingredient that is sadly missing in the secular educational system as well as with the modern parent. Although some might tend to disagree with the author's approach to discipline, yet his position is thoroughly Bible-based. *Certainly, even in the face of some disagreement, this work presents clear principles that can be applied in any family setting with success, if lovingly and wisely followed.*

As the author observes in his introductory "Author's Notes," there is real joy to be experienced in the parenting process, thus one must not lose sight of that joy while being consumed by responsibilities. My wife Ruth and I have experienced no greater joy than that resulting from sharing in the lives of our children, sharing in their growth, seeing them flower and mature according to our heavenly Father's design for their lives.

I see greatly needed principles, regarding the family structure and the process of parenting, in this book. Young and older families can study it with profit, applying the principles explored and avoiding the pitfalls revealed. *Although the author makes it clear that optimum success rests on the foundation of a sound Christian faith, yet the principles can be applied with profit by all.*

The solution for the lack of discipline that has resulted in the failure of so many young lives, even to the point of violence and death to which the author alludes, does reside in the hands of parents. The potential for failure looms large in the future unless parents assume and take back the responsibility for rearing their children. Public childcare, education, governmental programs cannot replace the role of parents. Thus the author rightly calls his readers to the renewal of the traditional family structure and values.

I commend this treatise to you, praying that, if parents, you will embark upon the journey of joy that will result in a destiny of great reward and joy. If not involved directly in parenting, you would do well to learn and share the insight revealed in this book with others.

Earl Radmacher, ThD
Chancellor Emeritus
Western Conservative Baptist Seminary

INTRODUCTION

THE JOY OF PARENTING

D r. Bruce Clatterbuck, Executive Director of *Next Generation Churches*, Conservative Baptist Association of Northern California and Nevada, upon reviewing the manuscript of this book, made these observations:

> *I appreciate your insights into child rearing and learning to understand your family. It has many helpful parts that I could see being used by young families to effectively minister to their children…. As you come to the latter parts dealing with the seriousness of parenting, I thought it might be help ful to put an introduction or a short chapter, **the joy of parenting**, balancing the responsibility and joy…, because sometimes young families are reading books on how to raise their children and are so concerned with doing it right (which they should be), they miss the fun of enjoying their children.*

Recognizing the wisdom of Dr. Clatterbuck's recommendation, I am including this introduction before dealing with the problem of a lack of discipline among our nation's children, emphasizing that the solution to the problem resides with their parents. As Dr. Clatterbuck observed, it is so important that the reader not be caught up in the responsibilities of parenting while losing sight of the joys and rewards that accompany this responsibility.

Our great Father God created the first man and woman, the parents of the human race, and then joy of joys, He ordained that man and woman join Him in the blessed task of bringing new life into the world, commissioning them to *"Be fruitful and multiply, fill the earth and subdue it."* (Genesis 1:28)

Thus begins this most fulfilling experience, bringing new life into the world and sharing in the growth of that life to maturity. While visiting new parents over the years, I have emphasized the privilege that God has given in permitting us to join Him in that creative process, emphasizing at the same time that the real task is yet to come, that of directing and molding that young life in such a manner that pleases our dear Heavenly Father.

Just contemplate the joy of parenting as young lives grow, form, and mature into something beautiful and unique – lives with unlimited potential designed for eternity. We create products and materials from the work of our hands, building a house, sewing a garment, carving an image, running a race, winning a game, cooking a meal, planting a garden, growing flowers, a thousand different things that produce great pleasure and a sense of satisfaction and fulfillment. Yet, how much more is the joy resulting from helping direct and form the lives of our children!

Give attention to these words from God, words that we will explore later:

> *Behold, children are a heritage from the Lord,*
> *The fruit of the womb is a reward.*
> *Like arrows in the hand of a warrior,*
> *So are the children of one's youth.*
> *Happy is the man who has his quiver full of them;*
> *They shall not be ashamed,*
> *But will speak with their enemies in the gate.*
> (Psalm 127:3-5)

Yes, *"Happy is the man who has a quiver full of [children]...!* The joy of child rearing continues to be an emphasis as we read from Psalm 128, verses 1 through 4:

> *Blessed is everyone who fears the Lord'*
> *Who walks in His ways.*
>
> *When you eat the labor of your hands'*
> *You shall be happy, and it shall be well with you.*
>
> *Your wife shall be like a fruitful vine*
> *In the very heart of your house,*
> *Your children like olive plants*
> *All around the table.*
>
> *Thus shall the man be blessed*
> *Who fears the Lord.*

Consequently, keep this promise of joy ever before you as you consider the problems that face our families and our youth, including the solution that will result when parental responsibilities are fulfilled in a timely manner. Do so and the task will ever be seen as a delight in the face of the finished product!

However, in considering the solution to the problems faced by the family and our youth, we must begin by considering and understanding the nature of the problems and their causes before we can fully understand the needed solution. **With these thoughts in mind, let us begin our journey together!**

Glennon Culwell
Scotts Valley, California

Chapter One

Setting the Stage

Denny Rowe, a 15-year-old sophomore at Columbine High School, Littleton, Colorado, sat on a knoll not far from the entrance to the school cafeteria. He suddenly saw Dylan Klebold, age seventeen, and his friend Eric Harris, both members of the Trenchcoat Mafia, dressed in their black trenchcoats, walking toward the cafeteria entrance.

As Rowe watched, one of them took off his coat, revealing what looked like grenades. As Rowe continued observing, either Klebold or Harris stopped 17-year-old Rachel Scott, engaging her in conversation for a moment. Rowe was horrified and paralyzed with fear as one of the black-coated pair took a semiautomatic rifle and shot her in the head.

Their next target would be Danny Rohrbough, age fifteen. This quiet lad was first shot in the hip. Rohrbough, stumbling and trying to run away, was killed with a shot in the back.

Thus began a day of tragedy and violence as these two teens, armed with guns and bombs, laid brutal siege to Columbine High.

Scores of students hid themselves in classrooms and closets, praying for deliverance. Five hundred kids were frozen in fear in the cafeteria; two freshmen girls hid in a bathroom;

another group of students huddled in terror in an upstairs closet for two hours.

Panic and confusion reigned. Dave Sanders, a popular 47-year-old teacher and football coach, instead of seeking safety for himself, circulated through the cafeteria and ran upstairs to warn students. Sanders suddenly found himself face-to-face with Harris and Klebold, who barbarously shot him in the chest.

As their rampage continued in relentless fury, they confronted a number of terrified students, asking if anyone was a Christian or believed in God. When Cassie Bernall stood, giving a positive reply, affirming her faith, these two callously shot and killed her.

Among those being targeted were Christians, a black student, and sports "jocks." During their rampage, they would be heard to order, "all jocks stand up."

When the tragic day came to an end, twelve students and one teacher had died at the hands of these two self-confessed members of the "Trenchcoat Mafia." An additional twenty-three students were wounded. Thirty propane tanks and pipe bombs were found planted in the school.

These two fanatic young teens reputedly were highly enamored with Nazi culture, unleashing their fury on Tuesday, 20 April 1999, Adolph Hitler's birthday!

Their plans were actually to destroy the school, kill all of those in the high school, and then spread their violence into the community and beyond. Harris allegedly wrote in his America Online profile, "Kill 'em all!!!" Klebold wore a shirt that said, "Serial Killer."

The events were as follows:

11:15 A.M. A call reporting shooting;

12:30 P.M. SWAT teams enter for room by room sweep of school facilities;

2:30 P.M. Police begin freeing groups of hiding students;

4:30 P.M. Harris and Klebold are found dead, victims of apparent suicide, corpses of ten of their victims surrounding them.

Why Columbine? We ask. Yet, here is only a point of punctuation in the continuing saga of terror on our school campuses, as well as in society at large. Here is but one manifestation of the raging epidemic of violence and accompanying hopelessness of our children. We are told that there has been a 300 percent increase in teen suicides since the 1960s, and 1,000 percent increase in depression among children since the 1950s.[1]

On 1 October 1997, Luke Woodham, age sixteen, of Pearl, Mississippi, killed his mother; then going to his high school, he opened fire, killing three and wounding seven.

On 1 December 1997, Michael Carneal, age fourteen, of West Paducah, Kentucky, shot three students to death at an early morning high school prayer meeting. Carneal apparently would have shot others had a student in the bible study group not grabbed him as he stopped to reload.

On 24 March 1998, Mitchell Johnson, age thirteen, and Andrew Golden, age eleven, both of Jonesboro, Arkansas, set off a fire alarm to draw students outside, and then started shooting, killing four of the students and a teacher.

On 21 May 1998, Kip Kinkel, age fifteen, of Springfield, Oregon, after killing his parents, shot twenty-four students killing two of them.

Why? Why Pearl, Mississippi? Why West Paducah, Kentucky? Why Jonesboro, Arkansas? Why Springfield, Oregon? Why Columbine?

Statistically, there have been 235 school associated violent deaths in the United States from 1992-1999. Sixty-six percent of those school deaths occurred in high schools, 17 percent in junior high schools, and 11 percent in elementary schools.[2]

Yes, "Death Goes To School!" However, this problem is only the tip of the overall crisis being experienced by children

21

of all ages. When we add such vexing dilemmas as drug use and abuse, alcoholism, gang warfare, teen promiscuity, unwed births, and any number of other problems, the crisis becomes overwhelming.

Consequently, when the term *"Columbine"* is used throughout this book, as the causes and solutions of the crises are considered, the term is used in reference to all of the problems affecting our youth.

Notes

1. *Time,* "What Can the Schools Do?" (3 May 1999), 2.

2. The Center for the Study and Prevention of Violence, University of Colorado and the National Safety Center, 21 April 1999.

Chapter Two

Why Columbine?

As we continue the saga called Columbine, we embark on a journey to see if we can discover the poison that produced this tragedy. What are the seeds of violence, and from where have they come, planted on our school campuses and in society, producing such a harvest of violence? A virulent plague of violence and hatred has infected many of our youth, leading to an epidemic of hate and death.

What has invaded the minds of so many of our children, and from where has it come? We will try to answer these questions and discover the solution, as we consider our subject—"Death Goes To School."

The Family under Attack

There may not be just one cause, but in general, *the major problem is found in the breakdown of the family.*

The family has been under severe attack during the past few decades, more than experienced in any other comparable time in the history of our nation. Family roles have been devastated and destroyed, resulting in a fragmentation of the family, leading to chaos, and creating a climate in which the Columbine tragedies are born.

The answer to our question begins to come into sharp focus in the 1970s, as reflected in the women's and children's liberation movements. Although the seeds for the destruction of the traditional family unit were being planted generations before, the harvest really begins to produce in the seventies.

Feminism

The Women's Liberation Movement, while having some admirable goals, nevertheless, has in a large part been designed to destroy the domestic role of the wife and mother. The goals of equal rights, equal pay for equal work, equal opportunity, all are noble and worthy of attainment.

However, while ostensibly endeavoring to attain such worthy goals, extreme feminists degraded the priority role of motherhood and the responsibility of parenting. The role of women, as we know, would undergo a radical, destructive change. The parental relationship would never be the same. The woman who chose a domestic relationship was viewed by the feminists as a downtrodden, second-class citizen. One had to have a career outside the home to be truly liberated. David Gelernter writes, "They had jobs, but feminists weren't satisfied; every other woman had to get one too. So they opened fire on homemakers with a savagery that still echoes throughout our culture. A housewife is a 'parasite,' [Betty] Frieden writes; such women are 'less than fully human' insofar as they 'have never known a commitment to an idea.' "[1] Such views have come to be an accepted norm, radically changing the structure of the traditional family.

That this was and is the design of extreme feminism, plus numerous other similar radical views, cannot be denied. Such an approach became internationally obvious as the United Nations proclaimed 1975 as "the Year of the Woman." A brief review of the process, plans, and goals of "the Year of the Woman" clearly exposes what they hoped to accomplish.

No effort is being made here to uncover a conspiracy, although there were and are insidious efforts involved. Yet it is significant that the move by the UN was introduced by the Women's Democratic Federation and was promoted and passed by the Communist/Socialist bloc of the United Nations. Their motives and views are easily determined by examining their official publication, a quarterly journal entitled, "Women of the Whole World," published in 1975 in communist East Berlin and distributed to 109 different countries, including our own.

The results are clearly enumerated in the resolutions passed at the International Women's Year meeting in Houston, Texas in 1977, first recommending what they called "Reproductive Freedom," which is just a fancy name for abortion on demand. Second, they advocated what was called, "Sexual Preference," another name for homosexuality. Third came the plank for "Non-Sexist Education at all Levels," in which they would endeavor to blur the differences in the roles of man and woman.

A fourth position deserves special attention. Finally, they advocated federally funded child development centers for *all* children. They recognized that, if the domestic role of the woman was to be changed, it would be necessary that the woman be liberated from domestic and family responsibilities, and if they were to leave their family and parental responsibilities, provisions would have to be made for someone to take care of the children.

As we will find, this fourth and final stand at the National/International Women's Year meeting will hold extremely significant importance when we come to consider "children's liberation."

We will discover that this radical change and view of the role of the woman in the family will be of major importance as we answer the question, "Why Columbine?"—Determining the causes of the lack of morals, standards, value of life, and inclination toward radicalism and violence.

25

The goal has been and is, as Gloria Steinem, former head of the National Organization of Women (NOW), said on "Meet the Press," 10 September 1972, "For the sake of those who wish to live in equal partnership, we must *abolish and reform the institution of legal marriage*" (emphasis added).

Steinem, in a further attack on traditional family values said in an address to the "Family Values Forum," held in Austin, Texas in 1997, "I think the first thing we need to reconsider about 'family values' is saying 'family' in the singular. That is a right wing trip altogether. The minute you say 'family' in the singular, it defines one kind of family as normal and renders all other forms peripheral or wrong. The truth is there have always been many, many different kinds of families, extended families, communal families, families in which, in the African tradition, children were raised by the grandparents, because it was thought that someone young enough to have a child was not wise enough to raise it. There have always been committed, nurturing relationships between men, between women and also chosen relationships, adopted relationships." She concluded by saying, "the idea that there is only one family form is really pure b—s—."

Children's Liberation

The United Nations proclaimed 1979 as the "International Year of the Child," with UNICEF the agency in charge of its implementation. Just as had happened in preparation for the Year of the Woman, once again the Women's International Democratic Federation would be in the forefront in preparing for the Year of the Child. They would hold an international seminar on 22 October 1977 in Prague, Czechoslovakia, with Marie Kabrhelova, Chairwoman of the Czechoslovakia Women's Union as featured speaker.

Kabrhelova would say:

> *Long before the representatives of all the peoples of the world in the UN decided to adopt the Declaration of the Rights of the Child and its ten principles, the socialist countries had gained vast experience in applying the ideas contained in the Declaration in everyday life. Socialism, the new social order, initiated 60 years ago by the Great October Socialist Revolution, which in such a decisive way influenced the development of mankind and the whole world has always considered its main duty to be to secure peace and devote all around care to the young generation. All the rights of the new generation to a harmonious, healthy and universal development of all children and young people are laid down in the Constitution of Socialist Countries. They are also again included in the draft of the new Constitution of the Soviet Union, which was the first country in history to solve all the problems of the young generation in such an inspiring way.[2]*

Such words as these leave no doubt as to the identity of the architects behind the International Year of the Child with its goals and methods for attaining "Children's Liberation." If, as Comrade Kabrhelova says, the children in socialist countries have already been "liberated," whom did they seek to liberate? Is it not clear that the US, along with other capitalistic nations, were targeted? Can we conclude that the USSR and other socialist nations were so altruistic that they were motivated in this effort to assist us? Were their objectives not suspect at best?

One should seek to identify those objectives at this point. The UN had adopted a resolution in 1959, under the same leadership, called the "Declaration of the Rights of the Child." The enemy is patient, for they would wait twenty years to implement the objectives of that declaration.

Another step towards the final objectives came when the UN General Assembly adopted two objectives on 21 December 1976. They stated in paragraph two of that proclamation:

A. Advocacy: provide a framework for child advocacy for special needs of children.

B. Action: programs for the children to be a part of all economic and social development. **Plans for the good of children change present child-parent relationships to state-child relationship.**[3] (emphasis added)

Here is the key to the entire program—change the parent-child relationship to a state-child relationship, i.e., take parental authority and responsibility and give it to the state! Is it not obvious that the UN had more on their minds than just helping "the poor children."

In illuminating their true motivation, one should examine the proposals and writings of the International Year of the Child. Let us scrutinize the goals of the International Year of the Child:

"1. Liberation from traditional morals and values."[4]
Just as Gloria Steinem said, "the first problem for all of us, men and women, is not to learn, but unlearn."[5]

In connection with this first goal, the IYC leaders would explain:

The real solution requires a fundamental change in the value commitments and the actions of the persons who control the public and private sector of our common life— parents and those whose decisions determine the life styles of other human beings.

Daycare is a powerful institution, a day care program that ministers to a child from six months to six years has over 8 hours to teach him values, fears, beliefs, and behavior.

This stated goal simply and clearly advocates taking children from parents and turning them over to state-controlled child care centers for training. How far along this path have these plans already progressed!

II. Liberation from Parental Authority. We recommend that laws dealing with rights of parents be re-examined and changed where they infringe on the rights of children, amendments should reinforce the primacy of the rights of the child.

In connection with this goal, one is reminded how humanist/psychologist Richard Farson gives a vivid account of his vision of the *"liberated child": freedom from punishment, freedom to vote, total sexual freedom, economic freedom, and others.*[6]

"III. The child must be protected from practices which may foster racial, religious, or any other form of discrimination."[7]

As Gloria Steinem, former head of NOW would say, *"By the year 2000 we will, I hope, raise our children to believe in human potential, not God."*[8]

Simply stated—children must be protected from parental influence regarding religion. Parents would be guilty of discrimination for teaching their children a religious preference.

"IV. Liberation from nationalism and patriotism." In connection with this goal it is stated:

> As long as a child breathes the poisoned air of nationalism, education in world mindedness can produce only rather precarious results. As we have pointed out, it is frequently the family that infects the child with extreme nationalism. **The school should, therefore, use the means described earlier to combat family attitudes that favor jingoism.**[9]
> (emphasis added)

What is jingoism? It might be defined as "extreme nationalism" which can be translated into "intense patriotism." Under this provision parents' efforts to inculcate strong patriotic, American principles and allegiance into the lives of their children would be subverted by the schools!

"V. Liberation from militarism."

A major theme that runs through this goal is that of disarmament. What is really being suggested is "peace at any price." Patrick Henry would remind us as he said in that little white clapboard church in Virginia, that we must not purchase peace at the price of being in chains, saying, "I know not what others may choose, but as for me, *give me liberty or give me death.*"

The secular humanists are rapidly attaining this goal, for Patrick Henry has a difficult time finding a place in today's history books.

"VI. Liberation from Capitalism."

The *UN Declaration for IYC* here advocates, *"a new international economic order, i.e. replace all capitalist economies with socialism."*[10]

Here are their six goals designed to establish the shackles of government control, including the control of the children! Are you beginning to understand the root causes that have led us to Columbine?

Methods and Measurements

If we are to roll back the floodtides that threaten the moral fabric in this country, we need to understand the methods designed to bring about the above stated goals and the measure of success that has already been attained.

First, they would work through NGO's, nongovernment organizations. One UN publication said, *"Nongovernment organizations, especially women's organizations, national planning, and other population organizations, welfare agencies, trade unions, cooperative, and religious bodies constitute important resources for development and vehicles of change. Their increased effectiveness depends on policies of governments and the increasing involvement of trained educated younger men and women."*[11]

Nongovernment Organizations (NGO's) include organizations such as the ACLU, the American Humanist Association, the National Organization for Women (NOW), Planned Parenthood, and of course many excellent organizations, including religious bodies. However, the excellent groups are only utilized as they conform to the humanist's goals.

Charlotte Bunch's comments in the opening plenary at the Center For Women's Global Fellowship, NGO Forum '95 on Women, are quite enlightening concerning the goals to be accomplished through the NGO's. In criticizing conservative efforts and values, she said, *"These conservative reactionary forces, whether nationalistic or religious or both, all seek to control women. This control is absolutely essential to religious or ethnic or cultural purity and identity."* Furthermore, she said concerning conservative family values, *"This has fueled the conservative backlash against women's autonomy and against all minority 'others' who might live differently, such as immigrants, gypsies, lesbian and gay people, etc. This brings us to the question of the very definition of the family. Feminists have been accused of being anti-family, but the conservative forces have continually narrowed the understanding of what the family really is."* Advocating global government, she said, *"Women must become more involved in seeking to develop global democratic structures for global governments."* She added, *"So as we enter into this NGO forum and send our messages back to Beijing to the government conference, one of those messages has to be that women in the world are watching the United Nations. In this week, at the NGO Forum, we must send forward to that UN conference next week in Beijing, the idea that we believe the world can be transformed by looking at it through women's eyes."*[12]

Second, they would achieve their aims through child development centers. The woman liberated from family and home must have someone to take care of the children, if they are to successfully rid themselves of their family domestic responsibilities.

One case in point, in California, the Santa Cruz County childcare centers pleaded for involvement in a public service spot over the local radio station. They said that, because certain families were hiring baby-sitters and keeping children in the home, this practice was damaging because of a lack of continuity in the lives of the children. In other words, they were saying that there would be more continuity in the lives of children if they could get them out of the home into child development centers.

Third, the IYC UN goals would be accomplished through the educational system. Mandatory public education would be a part of the monster that would engulf the American family. Child-rearing and the formation of children would be turned over to the state through its educational system.

The Success of Their Methods

Just how successful have their methods been? Consider just a few examples in measuring the efficacy of their methods in attaining their goals.

First, one sees evidence in the past regarding efforts of NGO's in liberating children from parental control, and reads daily of present efforts.

Even religious groups have fallen prey to the high-sounding goals of the humanists. Ministries emphasizing human potential, often at the exclusion of God, are little more than humanists dressed in religious garments—"Name it and claim it." "You can achieve what the mind can conceive." Such phrases fill their possibility messages, humanist principles cloaked in false Christian garments.

The measure of success attained by such NGO's as the ACLU, Planned Parenthood, NOW, the American Humanists, and similar organizations will be seen more clearly in relation to the second and third stated methods.

Second, their efforts in "liberating" children from the home and their parents, through child care development centers, show dramatic and obvious success. One would be shocked to discover that the proponents of child care out of the home would follow a Soviet Russia model. In a report favorable toward the Russian system of childcare, the *Los Angeles Times* published an article headlined, "U.S. Educators Study Soviet Child Care" (9 November 1978). The article noted:

> *With one of the most massive and highly organized childcare programs in the world, the Soviet Union has freed millions of mothers for work, and provided their children—from 2 months to 7 years of age—with a place to stay from 7 a.m. to 7 p.m., or even overnight.*

The *Times* reported this observation by Janice Gibson, a University of Pittsburgh professor who spent half a dozen summers in Russia studying kindergartens. Professor Gibson observed,

"*the U.S.S.R. is the first country with a mass centrally controlled preschool program available to all and designed to affect personality*" (emphasis added).

After a complimentary description regarding the benefits of a system which permits 80 percent of the Soviet women to work while the state "upbrings" their children, the article ends with this revealing paragraph,

"*the preschoolers are encouraged to cooperate with communal games and toys and to shun children who do not conform.*"

When this Soviet-style child care act was introduced on 15 January 1979, Senator McGovern said to his colleagues, "Mr. President, I am pleased to be a cosponsor of the 'Child Care Act of 1979.' In this, the International Year of the Child, I cannot think of a better way for Congress to demonstrate its commitment to children."

The NGO, the National Education Association (NEA), would then be funded with government grants in implementing this program, and the powerful teachers' unions continue in this role to this present time.

Since that time, government financed and supported child care has been a centerpiece in educational programs and budgets. Presidential budgets and programs and congressional legislation have featured new child care center plans and funding for child care, all facilitating removal of children from the home and freeing parents of their responsibility to train their children. There is a constant proliferation of child care centers governmentally funded, privately operated, and centers being developed by employers.

Third, the government endeavors to resolve all problems relating to children through the public education system.

For many years the humanist/socialist/feminist philosophy has permeated text books and institutions of higher learning. Dr. John Dewey, father of progressive education, was an original endorser of the "Humanist Manifesto" in 1933. The American Federation of Teachers Union has worked tirelessly in the past to lower the age of compulsory schooling to three years or younger. The National Education Association (NEA) endorses formal education at age two.[13]

Where schools were locally funded and controlled, they are now largely state and nationally controlled and funded. The system assumes control over the lives of children, usurping the role of parents at almost every level of training.

Of course the NGOs are there to keep the schools on the secular humanist path—the ACLU, the teacher's unions (NEA, AFT, CTA), NOW, Planned Parenthood, and others.

God has been removed, while homosexuality is promoted; condoms are dispensed, and moral values are undermined. Information is dumped on children with moral implications and standards forbidden. More and more money is dumped into the educational system, designed to solve child problems. Expansion and improvement of schools is high on every politician's agenda, with the outcome of many elections being determined by this one issue.

Discipline is passé'. Corporal punishment has been banished to the wood shed itself. With Dewey's views on punishment, children's liberation has done away with order in the schools. The inmates, along with the teachers' unions, are running the institution. Any real effort at control of students is condemned as "child abuse." Consequently, how can the schools be expected to avoid Columbine?

Summary

By now one will have concluded that the basic cause of Columbine and other related incidents is found in the breakdown of the family unit. Parents have all too often abdicated their responsibility for the training of their children, turning the responsibility over to the state.

A major responsibility for what has happened must be laid at the humanist's feet and the extremes of the feminist movement, charging them with destroying the domestic role of the mother. However, it should not be our intention to exonerate fathers and place the blame on mothers alone! The problem is that the roles of both have been distorted with the imbalance resulting from mom's absence and the state's intrusion, as it assumes responsibility for junior's care, direction, and education.

We will have more to say regarding this problem as we begin considering potential solutions.

Notes

1. David Gelernter, *Drawing Life, Surviving the Unabomber*, Free Press, 1997, 5.

2. Women of the Whole World, 1977.

3. UN General Assembly Minutes, 21 December 1976.

4. Saturday Review of Education, March 1973.

5. Feminist.com.

6. *Birthrights: A Children's Bill of Rights*, Richard Farson.

7. Principle 10, 1959, *UN Declaration of the Rights of the Child*.

8. Saturday Review of Education, March 1973.

9. *Toward World Understanding*, Book V, UNESCO in 1949, 58.

10. The UN Declaration for IYC.

11. Report of the World Conference of the International Women's Year, published by the United Nations, Number E76. IV, 1.

12. Center for Women's Global Leadership, NGO Forum '95, Opening Plenary, Charlotte Bunch.

13. *Today's Education*, NEA Journal, January 1969, 29-32.

Chapter Three

Proposed Solutions for Columbine

For twelve hours, 8-year-old Willie Jenkins clung to a cushion in the alligator infested Wacussa River and struggled to remember his grandfather's advice.

"His Pappy had told him before that if anything ever happened, to always hold on to a life preserver until help came," said Willie's uncle.

Willie and his grandfather, Robert "Pappy" Watson tumbled into the water when their fishing boat overturned. "Pappy" drowned as a result. Willie clung to his life preserver for twelve hours before his rescue, while gators swam around him through the night in this reptile-infested water.[1]

Our children desperately need something to which they can cling in these troubled times. Where will they find a "life-preserver" that will enable them to escape the Columbines of the future?

Proposed Solutions

Innumerable solutions have been proposed in recent months and years.

The public school has been hailed as the first line of defense. The school is seen as holding the solution to such problems under consideration. Thus, we hear the call for more and more money, for more and more teachers, smaller classes, better facilities, more training for teachers, and better equipment. In other words, the state will resolve our children's problems through its secular humanist school system. We are told in the UN Declaration of Rights of the Child:

> *The child shall enjoy special protection, and shall be given opportunities and facilities, by law and other means, to enable him to develop physically, mentally, morally, spiritually and socially in a healthy and normal manner in conditions of freedom and dignity.*[2] (emphasis added)

How can they do that when moral and spiritual values are excluded from the school? For example, under the guise of sex education, public schools present graphic sex and homosexuality as an acceptable life style, but as Representative Earl Schlep of Missouri said, "There's not a word in it about love or marriage or morals."

Neither the public school nor the state can solve this problem. In fact, they are at the very root of its cause.

Others suggest that *"gun control"* is the answer. Strict gun control or doing away with guns will resolve the problem, at least in part, they allege. As a result we see a veritable plethora of proposed legislation to control guns in the aftermath of Columbine, both on state and federal government levels.

These comments *are not* designed to argue for or against gun control in its various forms. Let us not be side tracked from the issue before us.

The point is, however, gun control in any form, desirable or undesirable, *is not* the solution to this problem. To take this route is treating the symptom rather than solving the problem. One is fearful that the issue is raised more for political gain, rather than really believing that such action will prevent violence.

Your author grew up in a gun culture, in which gun owner-ship was common, more so than today, yet one did not find students killing one another in school.

Donald Paul Gaston, a paroled felon, and cohort Matthew Mark Kozlowski were arrested in San Francisco for attempted murder, kidnapping, and robbery among other things. They were charged with kidnapping two victims, stabbing each of them fifteen times, and leaving them in a canyon for dead. One of the victims, a 15-year-old girl was also shot in the face.

Following the argument regarding gun control, how would one go about preventing a problem like this? Is the answer to control or outlaw knives?

The real solution is found in this statement in the news account, *"friends and relations of both Gaston and Kozlowski portrayed them as products of deeply troubled homes"*[3] (emphasis added).

Apparently, the problem and its solution are found in the home!

Harris and Klebold made bombs of butane tanks and pipes, following instructions from the Internet. The bomber of the federal building in Oklahoma City killed and maimed scores of innocent men, women, and children and destroyed the building with explosives made out of fertilizer.

If gun control will solve problems such as Columbine, must we not also ban the sale of butane tanks, pipes, the Internet, and fertilizer.

No, no! The solution must be found elsewhere.

Still others have placed the blame on Hollywood and video games for the violence portrayed. The answer in part, they say, is to clean up Hollywood.

Now, as attractive as that suggestion may be, that is obvi-ously not the solution to the Columbine problem, but once again deals with symptoms rather than the problem.

Hollywood has long portrayed violence, but the results seen today were not seen in the past. I recall my first sound movie,

"Powdersmoke Range," starring Hoot Gibson. Their guns, as they shot and shot at one another, would shoot a hundred times without reloading! The "powdersmoke" was so heavy at times that it was hard to detect details on the black and white screen. Yet, in spite of all of this violence, I did not go out and shoot others, nor did other youth viewing such films.

The gruesome details of violence today *are* so much more graphic than then. Hollywood morals and violence do need a house cleaning, but it is not the cause, nor solution, for Columbine.

Some Suggestions for a Real Solution

First, since the government cannot solve our problem, suppose we have the government do what it was designed to do! What is the role of government appointed by God? A brief overview of Romans, chapter 13 gives a quick answer. Here we see that government is charged with the responsibility for the administration of justice, and the purpose of that responsibility is twofold—for praise and punishment. We discover in verses three and four of that chapter that government's administration of justice is for praise of good works and punishment of evil. Fulfilling such a function would seem to inescapably include morals, would it not?

Yet, the excuse of politicians that they parrot is that you cannot legislate morals. In answer to such a position, former California State Senator H.L. "Bill" Richardson said, while speaking at a local prayer breakfast, "Don't you believe it. That's what legislators do." Just how many of the Ten Commandments are reflected in a large number of our laws?

Campaign finance regulations, legislation regarding discrimination, theft, murder, all involve morals—and the list goes on and on.

The government should get out of the family, cease assuming responsibilities delegated to parents, and get back to administering justice, for praise and punishment— *"ministers of God for good!"*

Second, parents should make their children their first priority, rather than the pursuit of materialism, wealth, and pleasure. Both mothers and fathers must spend time with their children, building in them godly values, high standards of conduct, and principles of morality.

Parents must not abdicate their responsibilities of training and discipline, turning their duties over to the school and child care programs and facilities.

Such an approach to child rearing, as being advocated will not work, a truth that has long been recognized. Wendy Dreskin focused on this truth over twenty years ago in an article entitled, "Growing Concern About Effects of Day Care on Kids." She would write in part:

> *Many child psychologists, educators, pediatricians, and even parents are becoming increasingly concerned about the effects of day care on the child. A child's capacity to love is formed in the first two years of life. The key is what psychologists call "bonding," a lasting attachment between the child and a loving adult—usually the mother. If this is missing, it may effect his ability to develop future human relationships.[4]* (emphasis added)

Selma Fraiberg, a professor of child psychoanalysis at the University of Michigan, says that, "except under ideal conditions, a daycare center cannot provide the relationship so essential to the child's intellectual and emotional development."[5]

May I add that neglect from parents, in building relationships with their children, will result in the same deficiencies.

Third, schools (public or private) *must teach moral values,* not abandoning them for the sake of humanist relativity. Conduct reinforced by discipline must be included if there is to be order in the school.

We will deal with these proposals and others in detail in

following chapters. For the moment, however, I suggest that we consider the foundational solution, if we are to experience optimum success.

Laying the Foundation

We must *pray*, first of all, or else God's will and way will escape us. We are told, *"Unless the Lord builds the house, they labor in vain who build it"* (Ps. 127:1). What has been said is not to suggest that, one not of the faith, cannot find valuable principles in this treatise. Anyone applying the principles found in this book will discover that they work wonders. Yet, how much better if they are applied under the direction and in the power of God!

Consequently, listen to Paul's words to young Timothy, as found in his first letter to Timothy,

> *Therefore I exhort first of all that supplications, prayers, intercessions, and giving of thanks be made for all men, for kings and all who are in authority, that we may lead a quiet and peaceable life in all godliness and reverence.*
>
> *For this is good and acceptable in the sight of God our Savior, who desires all men to be saved and come to the knowledge of the truth.* (1 Tim. 2:1-4)

Pray

First, we must pray. The Bible says, "Therefore I exhort *first of all.*"

That which is first in importance is prayer, "supplications, prayers, intercessions, and giving thanks." In other words, we are exhorted to employ every conceivable type of prayer or praying, with no exceptions!

For All

Furthermore, those prayers are to be for *"all men."* That means that we are to pray for all types of people, with no exceptions. No one is to be excluded from our prayers, believers or nonbelievers.

Again, those prayers are to include, *"kings and all who are in authority."*

Yet, our inclination is to exclude those we don't like from our prayers. Let us admit the truth of this statement.

Consequently, if we are to pray for *"all in authority,"* we are to pray for such men as the North Korean dictatorKim Il, or the Iranian ruler, just as Timothy would be expected to pray for the Roman emperor Nero, who was burning Christians alive to illuminate his garden parties, feeding them to lions, and other similar cruelties.

Furthermore, our prayers are to also include every official from the local school board, city council, state representatives, and federal office holders, including the President of the United States. We must admit that it is difficult to pray for some of these rascals, but only eternity will reveal what would happen if all of us did!

Why?

If we understand why such prayers are to be offered, the task will become easier. The purpose—"that we may lead a quiet and peaceable life in all godliness and reverence."

All of us desire to live in peace and tranquillity, to live a godly, reverent, and honest life. In doing so, we are not admonished to move to the mountains to find tranquillity, or to wait long enough to vote the rascal out of office, but to pray for all in order that there will be a climate in which such a quality of life can be lived.

Taking another step, we find other reasons why we are to pray for, *"kings and all who are in authority."*

First, because such is *"good and acceptable in the sight of God,"* God is pleased when you and I *first* pray, prayer that can result in this ideal quality of life.

The second reason is because He *"desires all men to be saved and to come to the knowledge of the truth."* The potential result of our prayers is the salvation of those in authority, accompanied by experiential knowledge of the truth.

Just imagine how such results would impact the problem we are considering, leading to a quiet and peaceable life rather than Columbine.

However, before we search further for such experiential knowledge of the truth, that which will reveal the true solution to Columbine, be reminded that we are to pray for *"all men,"* not just those in authority. We are led to ask, what would happen if parents were devoted to the task of parenting, investing significant times in offering *"supplications, prayers, intercessions, and giving of thanks"* for their children?

Notes

1. Associated Press, 12 April 1979.

2. UN Declaration of the Rights of the Child, Principle 2.

3. San Jose Mercury News, 8 July 1999.

4. Wendy Dreskin, Associated Press (Santa Cruz Sentinel), 17 June 1979.

5. Ibid.

Chapter 4

Stand Fast in the Faith

S atan, using all of the echelons of power in the world, at
every level of authority, community, state, national, and
international, is launching a severe and brutal attack. We find
that he has the family literally reeling on the ropes, raining
blow after blow through a radical form of women's liberation
and children's liberation.

The bell rang for round one at the International Year of the
Woman in 1975 and round two in 1979 at the International Year
of the Child, each designed to break and destroy the roles of
individual members of the traditional family.

Many times, Christian individuals and Christian organizations have not only fallen prey to these movements, but in many
cases have even endorsed them.

The director of a major Christian camp would headline his
article in the camp's newsletter, *"The Year of the Child,"* hail-
ing this effort as, *"a time to think deeply on the importance of
this emphasis." The* tone of the article could be construed as
giving unreserved endorsement of that proclamation, deceived
by its "high-sounding" goal, apparently expressing support for
this concept of "child liberation."

A Christian film producer, advertising films focusing on children, headed his advertising insert, "Year of the Child." He went ahead to write, *the year belongs to our children! The United Nations made it official by naming 1979 the International Year of the Child.* He would express concern over *"UN policies,"* but his comments would be interpreted as giving credence to this movement that claimed as its goal the "liberation" of children, and all of the radical concepts entailed in that proclamation.

The venerable American Bible Society, a stalwart old organization committed to the task of publishing and getting out the Word of God, sent out correspondence referring to "the International Year of the Child" in favorable terms. At one point they wrote, *"your special help in the Year of the Child means so much."*

Deceived? Misguided? Naive? Probably all of these descriptions are accurate, but point out that we must be alert, and uncompromising in our stand for the truth. In addition, these examples simply illustrate that even Christian NGO's are taken in by misleading goals and insidious language.

We have clearly documented that the two "liberation" movements, as illustrated in the 1975 and 1979 UN proclamations, were designed to destroy the parent-child relationships, virtually making our children wards of the state. Father does not know best as far as this movement is concerned, but Uncle Sam does, along with Uncle UN, mom and pop humanist, and all of the humanist family. They know what is best for our children better than we do as parents, and thus endeavor to impose on us what they think is best.

As we recognize this onslaught of Satan, and witness the widespread violence, such as that seen at Columbine, we must remain alert and careful, so that we will not be devastated, discouraged, and defeated in a malaise, feeling that all is lost without even engaging the enemy in battle.

We must *stand fast in the faith* if we are to win. That being true, let us begin looking more intensely at solutions to the problems that assault our children and family units—problems manifested in Columbine.

A Solution on the Nation—People Level

We must *stand fast* in assuming our family duties. Having abdicated our family responsibilities, we have taken what appears to be the easy route and have said, "let the government do it." A cartoon depicts this truth, showing a man being examined by a doctor who says smilingly, "I decided, rather than taking care of myself I'd let the government do it."

A part of the solution is to recognize that the government, including the public schools, cannot solve our problems. With that knowledge, we must reject the deception, turn a deaf ear to the harping of the politicians in search for votes, and take back the responsibility of rearing our children.

The school cannot rear our children for us, although they insist on trying to do so. In fact, the school system's attempts do more to undermine than to assist us in rearing our children. One failed effort is found in what they have erroneously called, "Family Life Education," in which they dump loads of raw sex on our children without teaching them responsible morals and values.

One case in point of how humanistic education deals destructively with the parent-child relationship is seen in Prentice Hall's school textbook on home economics, entitled, "Building Your Life." On page 123 the text asks, "*Are your parents old-fashioned? Do they ever embarrass you by the things they say or do in front of your friends? Are they often unreasonable? If so, perhaps you have tried to keep your feelings about it to yourself, but if you have talked to your friends about your difficulties with your parents, you have found that your friends have most of the same complaints that you have.*"

On pages 193 and 194 of that same text book we read, "*If you and your classmates would write on slips of paper the three things that bother you the most about your parents and then have a committee summarize the results there would probably be a large measure of agreement on troublesome traits in parents. Why do parents behave as they do? Is there any way you can help them to change?"*

As if that were not enough, the text adds on page 195, ***"but it is still aggravating to have to try to cope with parents who boss too much, who set old-fashioned and unreasonable standards and don't realize that a person has a right to some privacy in life"***[1] (emphasis added).

What do you think might be *"old-fashioned," "troublesome traits," "old-fashioned and unreasonable standards"* of parents as referenced in this textbook? Perhaps the sanctity of sex and the need for and value of abstinence!

A major conflict arose between parents, teachers, school administration, and some school board members in my community in recent years. The issue was whether the school would permit elementary age children to leave school to receive counseling without advice and permission from their parents.

I sat in the public board meeting where this issue was debated. The conclusion among school counselors and administrators, with agreement from a majority of the school board, was that the children could leave school for counseling without the consent of parents because *"children are not able to talk to their parents."*

Can it be any clearer that, in many cases, the schools claim to know better what is best for the children than their parents and actively seek to take over the task of child rearing, without moral or spiritual values!

On 28 June, 2001 then Surgeon General David Sacher urged parents and teachers to provide children with a thorough sex education that permits distribution of condoms or contraceptives in schools, including teaching that "mutually monogamous" or homosexual relationships are an acceptable alternative to marriage. Sacher did not limit a monogamous relationship to marriage because, as he said "marriage is not perfect." Properly interpreting the Surgeon General's words, he is saying that what we call "shacking up" outside of marriage is an acceptable alternative.

Every child needs to have equity of opportunity for sex education," Sacher said. In his interview over an NBC news telecast, Sacher admitted that many parents are equipped to provide such instruction, but was quick to add that "some are not." Who will make the determination as to who can and who cannot? The answer given by Sacher and his fellow humanist educators is, The school knows best! They will simply assume the responsibility for all, as Dr. Bruce Bagley, Chairman of the American Academy of Family Physicians said in relation to Surgeon General Sacher's report, *"The only way we're going to change approaches to sexual activity is through the school." (emphasis added)*

One solution is to get government and public schools out of the business of trying to usurp the role of parents, and for parents to be committed to rearing their children, while instilling spiritual and moral values. Any effort in this area, on the part of schools, should only be taken with the cooperation, permission, and the involvement of parents.

Training on the Individual Family Level

Here the church enters the picture as a part of the solution, standing fast in its teachings. The Church needs to impart biblical principles and examples regarding the family relationship. The flock needs to be nurtured on the Word of God. Furthermore, the Church not only needs to *feed the flock*, but it needs to *protect the flock*—teaching them to flee, as we find in 2 Timothy, chapter 2 verse 22 and resisting the devil as we find in James, chapter 4 verse 7.

However, the problem is that we find very little resisting of the devil, with no place to flee because the home, along with the Church, has promoted a ministry and message that actually appeal to the lusts of the flesh. We are beset with a "feel good faith," the Church only being relevant if the people "enjoy" or are made to "like it."

The flock basically wants to be fed, made to feel good, without producing any wool. People are encouraged to *"get,"* with little challenge to *"give."*

Local churches basically are out of balance, an example of this would be the law-grace or legalism-grace debate. Let us hasten to say that churches need to present a balance of the truth, for truth out of balance leads to error.

Truth is no more out of balance than in the law-grace debate. There are certain standards and laws of God that are to be obeyed. But if we openly call for obedience to those standards, teaching that people ought or ought not to do certain things, there are those who criticize and condemn and say, not so, for we are under grace and not under law.

We *are* under grace, justified through grace, and not by works. We do not work to gain acceptance from God. That acceptance is by grace and is unearned. However, if we teach that grace annuls the need to obey God, truth is out of balance. Grace and obedience are in perfect harmony. Grace can never be used as an excuse to disobey God.

We certainly do not want to be caught up in legalism, but we need to know what legalism is, if we are to balance truth and have balance in the Christian life. One, legalism is man trying to earn his salvation, or acceptance by God, through good works. And after doing so, two, trying to live the Christian life in his energy and through his own efforts.

With that information, let us see if we can find the truth in balance, recognizing that law and grace *are not* in opposition. However, keep in mind that such balance requires a personal relationship with Christ. On one side we see the *command*, under law, and on the other side an *appeal,* under grace, to do what is right. The law *commands*, but grace, on the other hand, *enables*. We see the command and then recognize that grace, and grace alone, gives the ability to obey that command.

On one side we have the *responsibility*, and on the other side we have the *ability*. So, under the commands of God we have the *responsibility* to do what is right, and under His grace we have the *ability* to fulfill our individual responsibility—truth in balance.

Jesus said, *"If you love me, keep my commandments"* (John 14:15). Obedience would be evidence of one's love for him, while in juxtaposition, it is love, a fruit of the spirit that would enable obedience—thus grace in action. As we read in Galatians, chapter 5, verse 25, *"If we live in the Spirit, let us also walk in the Spirit."*

So God has a moral law that is always to be obeyed in our walk or in our daily lives. Thus, the Church needs to follow the model of the Bible, teaching responsibility for right conduct as well as the abundance of blessings through grace.

There are absolutes regarding individual roles and responsibilities that are to be discharged by every member of the family. The Church should be dealing with these *hard* issues, not just tickling ears and seeking to entertain.

Strong Convictions

We must *stand fast* in our convictions, if we are to correct the course of the good ship "family values," strong conviction, and not compromise will be needed.

We have been guilty of permitting standards to slip in an effort just to get along. Our convictions regarding right and wrong have been compromised so as to avoid criticism in many areas, because we are not willing to be "branded" as extremists.

We stand in awe before such men as Daniel, Peter, and Paul. The real secret for their stature, along with their faith, was their depth of convictions that made them willing to die for them.

Daniel did not pause for a moment in making his decision to pray, even if it meant going to the lion's den! Yet, we live in such a time when convictions are so weak that we are not willing to stand, much less die for them. We are not willing to give up an hour of TV to pray. Jesus asked his disciples at Gethsemene, *"What? Could you not watch with Me one hour?"* (Matt. 26:40). Perhaps He asks the same while we "watch" TV!

The lack of convictions in our culture may be reflected in a suggested marriage contract reprinted in *Woman's Day* magazine. The oath read in part, "We are separate people with our own standards and they must never be fused into one, I cannot make you happy or unhappy, but I can make myself happy, I accept my ultimate aloneness and responsibility for myself."

With such shallow convictions, no wonder the divorce rate is so high. We are guilty, all too often, of substituting *preference* for convictions. We are asked to take a stand on an important, yet controversial issue, and our reply is, "I'd rather not, or I *prefer* not."

You see, that is a statement of preference, and not a statement of conviction. The forces opposing traditional family values have properly interpreted the lack of depth of our conviction and have felt free to challenge us at every point. Their success, coupled with our weakness, has led to the sorry state in which we find ourselves.

Why are convictions so important? Permit me to give three reasons, and when you see from where they come, you, too, will understand their importance.

"First, a conviction will not change." There are multitudes who avoid convictions who are unwilling to pay the price in keeping them, or who fear they will fail. Note: This test assumes perfection and is not fully valid, since from time to time with greater illumination convictions do change. However, the court in the case referenced, is dealing more narrowly with convictions relating specifically to those issues appearing before the court. There *are* basic absolute convictions based on the Word of God that should meet this test.

"Second, a conviction will be visible in daily living." James wrote that, *"faith by itself, if it does not have works, is dead"*

(James 2:17). Can we not also say that convictions, if they have no corresponding action, are dead!

"Third, a conviction will be consistent."

Do you wonder about the origin of these three requirements? They come from a Wisconsin Court ruling, *Wisconsin v. Yoder,* in 1972. The court ruled in that case that *freedom of religion applies if it is based on conviction.* These three things, just named, formed the basis of what the court ruled, constituted a valid conviction.

If freedom of religion rests on these three requirements in this country, we understand, then, just how important these three points are.

I have been told that there are those, in the field of law, such as the ACLU, who are carefully studying biblical convictions in order to challenge us in court, regarding the validity of our faith.

Here is the way the results would work:

Question: Do you accept the Bible as your source of authority, or do you believe the Bible? Answer: Yes.

Question: Does the Bible teach obedience to the laws of the land? Answer: Yes, unless it clearly contradicts duty to God.

Question: Have you exceeded the speed limit with your automobile recently? Or, have you ever fudged on your tax return?

Do you get the point? Although your answer might seem to be insignificant, it will prove whether you have a genuine conviction or not.

The *Wisconsin v. Yoder* ruling permitted no qualification. The court ruled—a conviction will not change; a conviction will be visible; a conviction will be constant.

Try this example: Does the Bible teach that the fruit of the spirit is, among other things, self-control? Do you believe in exercising self-control? *Have you overeaten lately?*

Your *done-lap*, that which done laps over your belt, will tell right away whether you have lived up to that conviction or not.

Do you understand the importance of strong convictions? In the case of *Wisconsin v. Yoder*, Amish parents were permitted to withhold their children from public schools *because they practiced their convictions.*

Permit me to ask you—could you defend the exercise of parental responsibility on the basis of your convictions? The Amish did.

We will never be able to reverse the trend toward Columbine until we exercise our God-given duties. And we will never exercise those duties apart from conviction that must meet the test. Anything worth living for is worth dying for!

Therefore, *stand fast in the faith!*

Summary

Parents are to reclaim the responsibility of rearing their children, taking that duty back from the state and its thoroughly secular humanist system. The state, through child care and various levels of education, cannot replace or fulfill the role of parents.

Neither can the church, but it can equip parents for the task, coming along side them in a joint effort, teaching scriptural values to the children, reinforcing the leadership of parents.

Finally, parents and other adults *must* serve as role models, exercising strong spiritual and moral convictions. The Bible speaks to us in this area, *"Watch, stand fast in the faith, be brave, be strong. Let all that you do be done with love"* (1 Cor. 16:13-14).

Notes

1. *"Building Your Life,"* Prentice Hall, 123, 193, 194, 195.

Chapter Five

Train Up A Child

As we have seen and experienced, the state has intruded upon and has interfered in the parent-child relationship, through both legislation and education. Government, including the public school system, has presumed to determine what is best for our children, insisting that they know more than parents what should be done in training children.

The state of New Jersey, with the support of NOW, enacted legislation years ago, adopting a penal code that lowered the age of consent for sexual relations to the age of thirteen! Their justification, supposedly, was based on the fact that children that young were sexually active, so they legislated and, by implication, condoned it. In taking that action, the state blatantly intruded on and interfered with the parent-child relationship.

Can we imagine parents saying to their 13-year-old daughter (or son), "Now dear, since you are thirteen and children become sexually active at that age, here is a packet of condoms. Go out and do your thing." That statement sounds ridiculous, doesn't it? Yet, the state's legislative action and their practice of condom distribution say the same thing do they not? Remember that they insist that they cannot legislate morals, nor can the school teach the same. Perhaps we might conclude, from word and deed, that they actually do legislate and condone, not morality, but immorality!

Many of you will recall the television series starring the late Robert Young, a wholesome series entitled, "Father Knows Best." Not so, says the state. They insist that children really cannot talk to their "old-fashioned" folks! The results are that the state assumes the responsibility, insisting they know what is best—a load of information with no moral or spiritual guide for application. Consequently, we wonder, "Why Columbine!"

Father (and mother) does (or should) know best. Thus, the solution to the problem under consideration involves getting the state out of family business, with the parents fulfilling their responsibility in training their children! Parents must cease yielding to the temptation to indiscriminately turn child rearing over to the state with its humanistic programs and principles.

Some may protest that what is being said does not apply to them. You may not have children, may be a grandparent, and may have already reared a family. However, we are reminded that everyone has the responsibility of knowing the truth and teaching that truth to others. We find in 1 John, chapter 2, verses 12 through 15 that little children, fathers, young men, and all ages are to be enlightened about the world system and impart that information to others.

We find in the book of Titus, chapter 2, verses 4 through 8, that the aged men and women are to teach the younger about home, husband, family, good works, sound speech, and good doctrine. There can be no question that every one of us has the responsibility of knowing and sharing the truth with others in every area of life.

With these thoughts in mind, I want us to concentrate further on the *solution to Columbine*. As we continue to explore the solution to this insidious threat against the family and the parent-child relationship, we will seek to understand precisely what that relationship should entail.

Our focus will be on Proverbs, chapter 22, verse 6, where we are told, *"Train up a child in the way he should go, and (even) when he is old he will not depart from it."*

We will extrapolate from those words the *principle, plan, and promise* involved in training up a child.

The Principle

The *principle* is discovered in these four words, *"Train up a child."* We find revealed here the parental responsibility to train their children.

Scripture after scripture reinforces this truth. We are told in Deuteronomy, chapter 6, verse 7, *"You shall teach your children."* Moving to the New Testament, we are admonished in Ephesians, chapter 6, verse 4, *"And you fathers, bring them (the children) up in the training and admonition of the Lord."*

As we have discovered, the genesis of our problem is that we, as parents, have abdicated this responsibility and have passed it on indiscriminately to others, including the state. (Author's note: notice that throughout this work, the word used is "we." This word is to be seen in its editorial form, for there are many who do not own the blame or guilt being levied. The concept of "societal guilt" is not valid.)

The Plan

"Train Up"

What is meant by the admonition to *"train up?"* That word "train" has some very enlightening meanings and applications in the original Hebrew language.

The word originally referred to the palate of the mouth, or the inside of the mouth. The word in its verb form was used, for example, in relationship to the training of a horse, or bringing into submission a wild horse. An untrained horse was brought into submission by placing a bit in its mouth.

I grew up on a farm and remember seeing varying kinds of bits that were put into the horses' mouths to control them. By manipulating the bit inside the mouth and at the jaws, the horse could be controlled and directed. Where instant control was needed for a saddle horse, a curved bit was used to bring pressure on the tongue and roof of the mouth, with leverage bringing instant pressure on the jaw. Other types of bits were used, with the situation determining the type.

We also find that this word was used to describe the practice of a midwife, who would, after the baby was born, dip her finger in a sweet solution and then massage the palate, the gum, and the inside of the mouth with the sweet solution. The infant would be caused to suck, inducing thirst and hunger.

Combining these two uses of the word we see, in relation to the horse, that it was used to describe bringing the horse into submission and in giving of direction. When used for a child, it described developing a thirst or hunger.

Furthermore, with a quick look at the Hebrew lexicon, we find that this word came to mean "to dedicate" or "to give instructions." Consequently, to "train up" a child involves bringing the child into submission, creating a thirst in the child, instructing, directing, all of these things involved in this admonition to "train."

A Child

What is the age of the child to be trained? What comes to mind when we hear the word *"child?"*

Normally, there comes to mind the image of an infant, or even a child of a preschool or early school age. Upon examination of the Hebrew word used here, we do not find this narrow meaning. As used in 1 Samuel, chapter 4, the word refers to a newborn infant. In 1 Samuel, chapter 1, its use is that of an infant who has not been weaned, while in Genesis, chapter 21, it refers to Ishmael before he was a teen. The word is used in reference to Joseph in Genesis, chapter 37, when he was seventeen. Genesis, chapter 34 uses the same word for one of marriageable age.

We recognize, then, that the word is broad in its meaning, applying to a child from birth until the time they leave home. We are to conclude, from such broad usage, that parents are responsible for training throughout this entire period.

The *principle* emerging is that parents are to build into their children, of all ages, a spirit of submission just as one would break and train a wild horse. They also are to create in the child a thirst and hunger to follow the right direction in life.

In the Way

Our instructions said, *"Train up a child in the way he should go."*

This statement seems to assume that we will know the course a child's life should take and then train that child accordingly. In other words, parents are not to hold their own preconceived notion regarding the course of their child's life and try to force the child into that mold, ignoring their individuality.

Here is one area where we have gone desperately astray. Look carefully at the little word "in"—"*in* the way he should go." What is being said is that their training is to be in keeping with, or according to *"the way he should go,"*—not just any old way, but *the* way that particular child should go! Not in your way, but in his way—*"the way that he should go."*

So, the reference tells us to train up a child according to *"his way,"* and that application makes a world of difference.

What is being said *is not* that the child should be permitted to do anything he or she wants to do. What then is meant?

What is being said is, if you desire to train up a child properly, you must get to know him, discover his way, and train him accordingly.

Clear as mud? If so, to discover the meaning of "way," examine Proverbs, chapter 30, verses 18 through 19, where we will find the use of that same word "way" in a different context. Solomon writes, *"There are three things which are too wonderful for me; the **way** of an eagle in the air, the way of a serpent on a rock, the **way** of a ship in the midst of the sea, and the **way** of a man with a virgin"* (emphasis added).

Obviously Solomon is not talking about a path or a road, but rather is referring to a characteristic, manner, mode, or tendency—the *manner* of the eagle as it flies, the *mode* or *method* of a serpent as it slithers across a rock, the *method* of a ship making its way through the sea, or the *method* of a man with a maid. These are all distinct, different characteristics that caused Solomon to say, they "are too wonderful for me" to understand.

In order to more fully understand this word, look further to its use in Psalm 7, verse 12 and Psalm 11, verse 2. In both of these verses of Scripture, the same word is used in verb form, referring to an archer bending a bow before shooting an arrow. We read in Psalm 7, verse 12, *"He bends his bow and makes it ready."* The Psalmist writes concerning the wicked in Psalm 11, *"the wicked bend their bow."*

The bend or bending of the bow is the same word translated "way" in Proverbs, chapter 22, and verse 6. Follow closely! The *"way" is the specific characteristic or tendency that God gives to the individual.* Notice this carefully! Every child, given to parents by God, has a *bent* already established by God. God has programmed the child's life in advance, giving him a special *"bent,"* way, a *"bend"* like the archer's bow. He is not like a piece of clay to be molded in our hands *as we desire*, but he already has a supernaturally bestowed bent in his life given by God, a divine design!

The parent, who desires to train his child correctly, discovers that *design* or *bent* and trains accordingly. Here is the way the amplified translation puts it, *"Train up a child in the way he should go, that is in keeping with his individual bent."*[1] What then do we actually do? We have a preconception of what the child should be like, and then we set out to make that child fit our preconceived mold. We ignore the individuality and uniqueness of each child, and we try to make them all alike.

Consider this tragic example. Dad says, "Junior is going to learn and excel in sports if it kills me"—and it may. Or mom may say, "Susie is going to excel as a musician if I die in bringing it to pass," and she may.

You see, we fall into the trap of seeking to make all of our children fit into a mold, forgetting their individuality, using the same approach with all of our children.

In our sports oriented society, and no one enjoys sports more than I do. Consequently we say that every boy must excel in at least one sport, and if he doesn't, something is wrong with him. He is abnormal. What a ridiculous notion!

I think about my own boys (now men). Christian, my oldest son does excel somewhat and plays well, at least in soccer and baseball. But when it comes to Andrew and Stephen, they could care less about sports. It was nothing unusual to discover Andrew in his room playing classical music so loud that the wall would be vibrating. And Steve, you might find him in the garage working on his friend's go-cart or perhaps constructing something with his hands. Stephen would often come to the dinner table, and I would ask, "Did you wash your hands?" You see he enjoyed making things, and when he did he would get his hands dirty—maybe grease from the go-cart!

The normal tendency in the world would be to say to Andrew and Stephen, why don't you play soccer or baseball like your brother Chris? Do you understand what is being said? Andrew liked to dress and be neat. Stephen liked to get his hands into the grease and make things. They are different. They have their own individual characteristics or bent, and they should be trained and developed accordingly.

Who said that one must play and excel in sports to be a fine American boy? Yet, we train our children according to such preconceptions.

Look at the scriptural example of Jacob and Esau, twins, born at the same time, one holding on to the other's heel. Esau would be the very essence of the macho man today, a man of the field who preferred his father. Jacob preferred to be at home to work around the house, and he preferred his mother. I have heard people suggest, and I may have even done so myself, that Jacob was a sissy. But if I ever did so, I want to apologize today; because I ask you to remember how when Jacob fled from his wrathful brother, fleeing for his life, he met Rebecca, the light of his life. Thus, we remember how he intervened on her behalf in watering the sheep, intervening for her against those other shepherds who would bully Rebecca. That wasn't the action of a sissy. You see the truth was that Esau and Jacob had different bents; they were different characters, though they were twin brothers.

Perhaps the truth expressed here explains much about Harris and Klebold at Columbine. There was such an emphasis on sports in school, and Harris and Klebold, having no interest in sports, would be observed as being odd. Would this not explain, at least to a great degree, their anger toward "sport jocks?"

* * * * *

You will have observed by now that the training being considered is not exclusively spiritual training. Yet, we have normally applied this text only to the spiritual when it

actually deals with the total life, dealing with the "natural" characteristics given at physical birth, programmed by God, with great significance in relation to the vocational life. Thus, the need to study, observe and know our children so as to know their bent.

Check out Moffat's translation of Proverbs, chapter 22, verse 6, *"Train a child for his proper trade, and he will never leave it, even when he is old"*[2] (emphasis added).

Perhaps Moffat narrowed the translation too much, extreme in one direction, while Verkuyl is perhaps overly broad. Verkuyl translates, *"Educate a child according to his life requirements; even when he is old, he will not veer from it."*[3]

The point being made is that we have consistently misapplied and misinterpreted this portion of God's Word.

The Promise

Having trained up a child according to his "bent," God makes this promise, *"and even when he is old, he will not depart from it."*

What Is Not Meant

At this point, we should consider what the promise *does not* mean.

The prevailing application, based on an improper interpretation of the principle and plan, is applied something like this—if parents will have their children in Sunday school and church regularly, if they make sure that they are involved in church related activities, if they have family devotions, and teach them biblical principles and encourage that they be followed, they may go astray, sow some "wild oats," but when they are old they will return.

In other words, they say, if they are trained and taught how to live by the Bible, even if they rebel and go astray,

they will return. This passage really makes no such promise, since the training involved is more in the natural realm,
according to their bent or character.

We repeatedly see devoted Christian parents who set
exemplary examples for their children, who have given their
children constant Christian instruction, who have had them
in Sunday school and church regularly, and yet those children
have lived immoral lives, and in some cases have continued
to do so throughout the balance of life.

When such as this happens, it seems as though God has
gone back on His promise because they did not return to
the way they were trained. How can one explain this seeming failure of an unfailing God? The answer—this is not the
meaning of the promise at all!

The Meaning

What does the promise mean? Notice that the original
says, and we emphasize the word,

"even when he is old he will not depart from it." (emphasis
added)

The promise doesn't say that the child will rebel, go out,
and "sow wild oats," but rather, **"even** when he is old he will
not depart." When the child is trained properly according to
his "bent," *even* when he is old, he will not depart from that
training.

Actually the word "old" means *"hair on the chin"* or *"one
with a beard."* Thus, the term old, as used here applies to the
age when the boy grows a beard, or when he reaches maturity.

The promise is—when the proper training is given, as
referenced in the verse, even when the child matures and
begins to grow a beard, he will not forsake that training.

Do you realize that one of the greatest causes for discon-
tent and rebellion comes from a lack of fulfillment in voca-
tion? When the individual has not found his or her niche,

they feel like a failure, and their view of every facet of life is impacted negatively. You see that the bent and training impacts the total life. I sat visiting with a friend who runs a rather large print shop. As I asked him about his business, he said that one of his greatest disappointments, experienced recently, lay in the number of skilled employees who had worked for him a long time. They were discontented and quitting to go to other jobs. We see this action often, as people run from job to job, not having discovered their niche in life, that is, their bent.

I preached a message on this topic some years ago and a man came to me afterwards, who had put in years towards retirement working for the post office. His job was pure drudgery. He hated to go to work every day. As a result, Joe said to me, "Pastor, thanks for that message. I've always wanted to do auto body work, and after that message I'm quitting the post office to do what I enjoy." Years have passed, and Joe goes to work daily, enjoying his work and his life.

Here is a reason we see college students changing their major so often. Parents have failed to train them in finding and developing their bent!

A Lesson for Columbine

Apply what we have been learning to Eric Harris and Dylan Klebold, "villains" of Columbine.

Other students observed that they were different, and so they were. They possibly fell into the classification of being "nerds," and were treated accordingly. While the sports "jocks" were being idolized, Dylan and Eric would feel left out and even rejected.

Is this consideration a reason why they targeted the "jocks" in their reign of terror? They write:

Upon being hazed, we read: Some of the Trench Coats tried to ignore it, but some snarled back, and one reportedly flashed a shotgun at his abusers in the park. They made a video for class, a tale of kids in trench coats hunting down their enemies with shotguns. The graffiti in the boys' bathroom warned: Columbine will explode one day. Kill all athletes. All jocks must die.[4]

Were Harris and Klebold victims who fought back, having been shunned because they were "different?"

We will find that the problem goes much deeper than that, but for the moment, just suppose that Eric's and Dylan's parents had identified their unique bent and had taught them that it is alright to be different. After all, everyone isn't designed to be a sports "jock."

Summary

Suppose we make two short observations as we conclude this chapter.

One observation, if we are to take back our families and prevent further destruction of the family unit, parents must get acquainted with their children, and begin fulfilling their responsibility of training, developing them both spiritually and naturally, according to God's design.

How interesting to read about the age of Dolly, the first cloned sheep. The "cloners" were surprised to find that her age was not just the time since she was cloned, but actually the age of the sheep from which she was cloned. Her composition, including her age, was programmed into that one cell from which she came. I believe that every man, woman, boy, or girl is "programmed" by God. The bent begins when the two cells combine into one at the very point of conception. There the bent begins, waiting to be discovered and developed by mom and dad!

One of the greatest joys you will ever experience, as a parent will be in developing the life of your child according to God's bent, plan, or design. I found the following words in my records, not knowing the source of their origin:

> *To love my child more truly everyday,*
> *to lead her unto Christ, the living way,*
> *to hide within her heart God's word and pray*
> *the Lord will save from sin*
> *bringing forth new life within,*
> *This is my joy, to teach my child*
> *by precept, word, and deed*
> *a noble, true, and worthy life to lead*
> *to serve her Lord and mankind in their need.*
> *Be patient, tender, kind, inspiring heart and mind.*
> *This is my joy.*
> *Then Lord, thou biddest me enter into rest*
> *of all earth's trophies, this one is the best*
> *and of all life's work and worth*
> *it is the test to bring my children in,*
> *this crowns my joy. (author unknown)*

The greatest fulfillment for a parent is to properly see their children's lives trained the way that God has designed them.

A second observation, we, you and I, must recognize that God has a bent, a plan, a design for each of our lives. We could be seven or seventy, never having discovered that design, or perhaps having rebelled against it. That being true, life may have lost much of its joy and meaning. I observed a bumper sticker with these words, "I go to work and then I die!" Has life no more meaning than that? The tragedy is that those involved in the Columbines may be so afflicted.

I discovered my bent and God's fuller plan for my life when I was nearing the age of thirty and my life has been enriched and given real purpose. You need to discover yours, too, if you have not. It is not too late, no matter what your age. You may be able to do nothing at this time of life, about your vocational bent, but it is never too late while you live to discover God's greater plan for your life.

Notes

1. Amplified Version of the Holy Bible.

2. James Moffat, *"A New Translation of the Bible,"* (London: Hodder & Stoughton)

3. Gerrit Verkuyl, Ph.D, *The Holy Bible, The Berkley Version* (Grand Rapids, MI: Zondervan Publishing House, 1959).

4. *Time,* 3 May 1999, 2.

Chapter Six

Knowing Your Child's Bent

"**D**on't look a gift horse in the mouth," so an old saying goes.

What we have been sharing with you in previous chapters is a "gift horse that you should look in the mouth," scrutinize carefully, and after having done so, reject the gift. Of course, we are talking about the humanistic approach to rearing children, manifested in what is called women's and children's liberation.

Much of the language used in those movements is couched in beautiful terminology, describing wonderful benefits which all should desire. Who could possibly be against a movement to give women equal opportunity with men, equal pay for equal work, and eliminate discrimination? Who could possibly be against an effort to eliminate child abuse?

Yet, in spite of all the high-sounding phrases and seemingly noble motives, we have documented results that show us that these movements have been used to tear down and fragment the traditional family unit. With individual family members liberated from their proper roles, no family unity remains, and the security of the relationship is lost.

Robert P. Dugan, Jr., former Director of the National

Association of Evangelicals (NAE), suggested that the UN Year of the Child was designed in such a way that it would fragment the family. Dugan said, *"American families would be wise to look the gift horse of government assistance in the mouth. Christians should be wary of the possible damage the International Year of the Child programs could do to the family as biblically portrayed."* Mr. Dugan added, *"Many of the originators of the UN resolution are humanists, socialists in the classic sense. Quotations from their writings indicate that they would love to tear down the traditional family structure, making the rights of the children primary over the rights of parents."*

As we look at the example of the Swedish "No Spanking Legislation," we recognize the pattern that has subjected many parents to the tyranny of their children. We are living *beyond* Orwell's *1984*, as there are built into existing regulations provisions for the children to report on their parents who have offended them.

A provision was made in the Swedish legislation for an emergency phone watch for children to report acts by parents twenty years ago. The law prohibited "any act which for the purpose of punishing, causes the child physical injury or pain, *even if the disturbance is mild and passing*" (emphasis added). This law not only prohibited physical pain in punishment, but punishment on the psychological level as well.

Such provisions enable children to literally tyrannize their parents, if they so desire. Not only that, if a teacher or social worker discovers evidence of punishment, they can activate the tyranny on their own. No wonder we read today about children suing their parents!

Can you just imagine saying firmly to your 5-year-old son, "go to bed," and he responds by looking at you and saying, "why don't you make me go to bed, and he might continue, "if you lay a finger on me or speak harshly to me again, I'll call the cops."

The extreme view of children's liberation, as advocated in the UN proclamation of "the Year of the Child" in 1979 and by their fellow travelers has led to a rash of extreme efforts by government agencies prosecuting supposed child abuse cases, efforts seemingly designed to validate their support of "Children's Rights." Cases in point, where child witnesses were coached and testimony was apparently fabricated, include: the notorious Amirault case in Massachusetts; the Wenatchee, Washington fiasco; the Robert Kelly case in Edenton, North Carolina, and the miscarriage of justice in the prosecution of Grant Snowden, a Miami police officer. The majority of the charges in these cases have been exploded and a number of sentences overturned. Yet, these actions serve to illustrate the dangers posed when a government goes to such efforts in advocating the extreme views being proposed in so-called "children's rights," making popular the action designed to cause adults to look like the "bad-guys"—often with political aspirations involved.

What I have just written sounds so ludicrous that it is almost humorous, but that could happen under some of the so called "children's liberation" provisions in existence. Parents, under prevailing laws and regulations, are virtually denied control of their children.

These implications establish how important it really is to examine the problem, as we have been doing, and discover the solution in a Christian alternative.

Train up a Child

We discovered earlier that we are "to train up a child in the way he should go" (Proverbs 22:6). Furthermore, we found that this training was all-inclusive, covering every area of life, spiritual, physical, and vocational.

In addition, we came to understand that God has given

every individual a bent or design, has programmed certain tendencies into their lives. Not only that, but we are promised that when we train the children according to God's design or their individual bent, they will not depart from it!

Knowing Your Child's Bent

In the light of these instructions, and that promise, the first question that should come to our minds is, "How can we determine God's design for our children?" "How can we know the child's bent?"

Three Characteristics

We recognize that there are three different characteristics relating to the bent or design of every child, characteristics one must know if one is to successfully train their children.

One, every child has a bent toward good, designed or given by God, which forms the child's basic personality.

Two, every child has a bent toward evil inherited from Adam, a sin nature. The Bible clearly indicates that the child has more than a bent, but has inherited a sin nature. As the Bible tells us, *"There is none righteous, no not one"* (Romans 3:12).

Three, every child has several specific characteristics or tendencies inherited from his or her human family.

The Bent toward Good and Evil

God bestows the characteristic toward good; while the bent toward evil, the sin nature, is inherited from Adam. If we are to exercise our God given responsibility and train our children properly, we must know and constantly keep in mind what their bents are.

Toward Good

Suppose we begin by establishing the case for the child's God given bent toward good. We find a supernaturally inspired, beautiful expression of this design in the 139th Psalm, verses 13 through 16. Let us analyze some of the words, promises, and truths that are discovered there. As we do, we will begin to understand how God goes about bestowing His design or bent upon the individual.

First, observe verse 13 where David, the sweet psalmist, is speaking. Focus on these words, *"For you formed my inward parts."* David is saying, "You God, and no other one but You, formed my inward parts." God did the forming from the very beginning. It did not come to pass through some evolutionary process, or by chance, or through natural selection, nor even Mother Nature, but God, and God alone formed our inward parts.

Furthermore, the word *"formed"* means to *"originate,"* while the word for *"inward parts"* comes from the Hebrew word meaning *"kidneys,"* referring to the vital organs that are necessary for life. The psalmist tells us, God alone originated all of our vital organs, without which life would not be possible.

Next, David continues in verse 13 and adds these words, *"You covered me in my mother's womb."*

The word *"covered,"* translated *"weaved"* in the authorized translation, means to *"knit together."* God has woven, knitted the child from conception, in the uterus, before birth, with his or her own distinct design, according to God's desire.

As has been previously stated, God programs the total design of the child the moment the male sperm unites with the female ovum, forming that first cell. Every feature of that child's life is programmed and set from conception—gender, physical attributes, mental capacity, talent, potential, and personality.

If the computer scientist can design a microscopic chip, which will perform millions of functions, would an all-powerful Creator-God find it difficult to include every facet of an individual's life in one cell? Thus, from the moment of conception, the child's total bent is formed.

Although David knew nothing of computer science, his phrasing regarding God's miracle work said it all! Consequently, this great truth would cause David to break out in worship, as it were, lifting his voice in exaltation to God in thanksgiving, saying in verse 14,

"I will praise You, for I am
fearfully and wonderfully made;
marvelous are Your works,
And that my souls knows very well."

However, don't stop reading here. David continues by saying,

"My frame was not hidden from You,
When I was made in secret,
And skillfully wrought in the lowest parts of the earth."

Those words, *"my frame,"* means *"my bony substance"* or *"bones,"* literally my bony frame or skeleton.

Take all of these words and magnificent truth is enunciated. The words *"Skillfully wrought"* picture, in the original Hebrew text, a finely woven cloth with variegated colors and design. The same word is used in Exodus, chapter 26, verse 36 in describing the curtain or door to the tabernacle.

"You shall make a screen for the door of the tabernacle,
woven of blue, purple, and scarlet thread, and fine
woven linen, made by a weaver."

The word "weaver" means a "variegator." Thus we have a picture of a finely woven material, a beautiful, magnificent material of variegated colors. Here is the word that David uses in describing how he was skillfully wrought in the depths of the earth.

So, God puts us all together, weaving a magnificent pattern, indescribable colors, unique, a pattern all our own in the depths of the earth—the words "depths of the earth," meaning literally a place of protection or security, a reference to the womb of the mother.

As an aside, we would recognize that the womb is a sacred place, off limits for all, including the abortionist. For every pregnant woman, there should be a sign on the womb that says, "off limits—God is at work!" Mother Nature is not at work. Man is not at work. This work is God's doing and is "off limits" for everyone else—a wonderful, protected place of security. God, like a master weaver, fashions and forms the child like a magnificently colored piece of tapestry, with its own design. There is not another like it. No one else has the same pattern, even his fingerprints, or his DNA. Every child is beautifully unique.

Before departing from this magnificent passage, we must consider Exodus' verse 16 also.

"Your eyes saw my substance,
being yet unformed,
and in Your book they were all written,
the days fashioned for me,
When as yet there was none of them."

God watched over us in our prenatal, embryonic, *"unformed substance,"* like a master designer, carefully designing according to His plan, overseeing our formation in order that we would be made just as He had designed, in accordance with His plan.

"And in your book they were all written, the days fashioned for me, when as yet there was none of them." Every child a book, and that book records the days prescribed by God alone, recorded there before conception— *"When as yet there was none of them."*

You see, God has a special book for every child, and those books are designed and prescribed by God and God alone. How wonderful that God placed five of those books in my family, in living form. Their names are Shirley, Janet, Christian, Andrew, and Stephen.

Every one of them is to be seen and studied as an "original." We see jewelry" hand-crafted by Charles," clothing that are "originals by Pierre." What we are illustrating is that, every child is crafted, designed by God, and is an original!

I thought of this truth one Wednesday evening in an awards ceremony for a girl's club in our church. Let me see if I can recall the words of a song they sang:

I have a little sister who's
not at all like me.
She can write a lovely poem
but I can climb a tree.
My brother, too, is different
with freckles on his nose,
When my questions needed answers
he's the one who knows.
That's why He made me special,
I'm the only one of my kind,
God gave me a body
and a bright healthy mind.
He had a special purpose
that He wanted me to find
So He made me something special
I'm the only one of my kind.(author not known)

Isn't that marvelous? Every child is special, one of a kind. There is not another one who fits that design, that plan. God crafts and designs the child before conception, and programs that design at conception, watching over the formation of the child in his or her development. Listen to this reading of our passage in Psalm 139 with an expanded meaning suggested by our previous considerations:

You, God, and no one else, originated my vital organs, my innermost being, You wove me in my mother's womb. I thank you for keeping me and making me in such a fearful and wonderful fashion. Wonderful are your works. My skeleton and bones were not hidden from you when I was made in that wonderful concealed place of security, when all of my parts were woven together like a magnificent variegated colored tapestry. Your eyes watched over me while I was only an embryo, and even before my conception, in Your book my days were described, that would shape me into the kind of person you want me to be."

Study and Know Your Child

The wise parent will recognize that every child is a gift from God, uniquely designed and will train that child according to that design in every aspect, every characteristic. The child may be short or tall, may be broad or thin, may be intellectual or artistic, may be athletic or mechanical, may be sanguine or choleric, may be melancholy or phlegmatic, and may be sensitive or calculating.

Parents are to observe and study their children, determining and understanding their bent. Body language, mannerisms, habits, and activities, all tell parents a little about their children. Study the children physically, spiritually, emotionally, in every way, getting to know them by observation and by conversation.

Then, in prayer and study of God's Word, train that child

according to the bent given by God and learned by you through intense study and observation. Parents who do that will have no tragedies with the Eric's and Dylan's of this world!

Magnify Their Bent

Once we study and know our children, we must let them know that their bent is special. Give them approval. Help them to be the very best according to God's design. We must not try to make something of them that conflicts with their natural bent.

We have observed how one emphasis in our culture is that everyone must be skilled in sports, and if not, something is wrong with them. Well, another ridiculous view abroad is that every child must go to college and get a degree, the feeling being that no one can succeed otherwise.

I told you about my son Stephen, how he liked to work with his hands, making and fixing things. Well, when Stephen graduated from high school, he went briefly to a trade school. His mother and I committed the cardinal sin by telling him that he didn't have to go to college! You see, we had studied and learned Stephen's bent and realized that a college degree was not what Stephen needed.

Well, Steve went to work, working with his hands. He is a skilled metal worker today, successful and earning a good living wage, happy in his work. Steve has said to me a number of times, "Dad, thanks for not pushing me go to college, for permitting me to pursue the work I like."

As an aside, our public school system has contributed greatly to the problem, amplifying and emphasizing the need for college, focusing on preparing everyone for a higher education, called a "college prep" curriculum. We desperately need schools in skills, where children with different bents can properly develop. If such schools are not possible, the emphasis should be changed, and some different opportunities in specialized courses should be given. How different this view is from that promulgated in our humanistic school systems. In the same vein we have been considering, we find humanist educators insisting that every child must be subjected to sex education, under the assumption that education and information will cure sexually related problems. Thus they dump a great load of raw sexual information indiscriminately on every child alike. Now one child may be able to cope with that information and get by all right, but another child may be deeply sensitive, and as a result have his or her life scarred.

On the other hand, the probability is that a number of the children will take the information, not accompanied by moral instruction, accept what they hear as being tacit approval of sexual activity, and begin in indulgence.

Once again, the tragedy is that the school insists on assuming a role that should be the privileged right of parents, who are in a position to know junior's bent!

We started out, in this section, emphasizing that the individual child's bent needs to be magnified, and the child needs approval. When I was in school, for years I was the smallest kid in my class. I resented that, beaten down, not liking that distinction. If my parents had only taught me that I was a special design by God, a very special original, and that my size was part of that design, the emphasis would have made my outlook completely different. Rebellion in children is exacerbated when the parent does not understand what the bent of the child is, and fails to appreciate the child for who he or she is. During these "little days" of my life, my parents tagged me with a nickname that I deeply resented, that contributed greatly to a feeling of a lack of approval. It was only by the grace of God that I did not rebel. To their credit, my parents were faithful in giving me Christian training.

Again, parents often try to force an interest that is not

79

there, trying to force the child into being something according to their own or society's preconceptions. When the child fails to conform to that preconception, parents see that failure as a flaw, acceptance is missing, and rebellion results.

For example, here is a hulking football player, who has a son who is deeply sensitive and artistic. He looks at that son in the light of the values of the day, determines that there must be something wrong, and ends up trying to make that son something God never intended him to be.

Do you understand the difference between the humanist approach and what I have chosen to call "a Christian alternative?" The humanist presses all children into the same mold, not understanding God's different endowments on different children. They feel that they can solve all problems with more money, more teachers, more classrooms, more, more, more.

The "Christian alternative" recognizes that the key ingredient is the role of the parents in teaching their children, including the training of their children in character!

The Bent toward Evil

Just as every child has a tendency toward good, every child also has a tendency or bent toward evil, coming as an inheritance from Adam.

If we fail to recognize that bent, we will never understand the reality of warfare between good and evil, and thus fail to recognize one of the primary reasons why the child is not cooperating.

While the bent towards good, given by God, must be developed, the bent towards evil, inherited from Adam, must be broken.

If we address one apart from the other, failure is inevitable. You see, the child is born into sin, having inherited the sin nature from Adam as the head of the human race. As the

Apostle Paul tells us in Romans, chapter 5, verse 12,

"Therefore, just as through one man (Adam) sin entered the world, and death through sin, and thus death spread to all men, because all sinned."

Proper Training Necessary

Proper training must include the remedy to the sin problem. The only real and effective remedy, to the problem of sin, is found in a spiritual new birth through faith in Christ as Savior.

One may teach good standards of conduct in dealing with the sin nature and problem, an approach much better than no training at all. However, any success will, apart from Christ, be only partial and incomplete.

The Bible tells us in Psalm, chapter 51, verse 5, *"Behold, I was brought forth in iniquity, and in sin my mother conceived me."*

Those inspired words enumerate the truth, along with Romans, chapter 5, verse 12, that every person ever born, other than the Lord Jesus Himself, has a sin nature. Consequently, the parents never successfully train a child if they refuse to believe or accept that the poison of sin runs through every person's veins.

It's here that the humanist goes astray, insisting that every person is essentially good, and because of that inherent goodness, discipline is not needed. The child must be free, which includes freedom from parental authority. Because of this perceived inherent goodness, as seen by the humanist, discipline and punishment are viewed as not being needed, a view leading to the removal of corporal punishment from both family and school. If corporal punishment is administered in our society, it most often is branded as "child abuse."

Summary

Think with me briefly, and wrap it up in these words. Every child has a bent toward good, a design given by God that requires training and development. On the other hand, every child has a bent toward evil, inherited from Adam in the sin nature, and that bent requires correction.

If we see our children as having one bent without the other and fail in either development or correction, we will fail, with potentially disastrous results, possibly even leading to something like a Columbine. Balance between development and correction is essential.

Chapter Seven

Breaking Adam's Bent

O ur families have been under vicious attack by human- ist social engineers, seeking to alter and realign the family unit through extreme manifestations of women's and children's liberation. Those efforts have fragmented the family, leading to undisciplined children, with results simi- lar to those seen in Columbine, and other circumstances of greater or lesser degree.

We have been dealing with the cause and solution of the Columbine conduct, resulting in a proclivity toward hate and violence. That conduct is an attack against the traditional family unit, its roles, and values, and ignores the necessity that one must be born again by faith to really cope with the sin nature.

That attack, so evident in the women's and children's liber- ation movements, is directed against the parent-child relation- ships. The efforts may be well intentioned, but are graphically exposed as being misdirected. As some are heard to say, "the road to hell is paved with good intentions." Thus, no matter how good the intentions may have been, which is subject to question, they obviously have been destructive and have born bitter fruit—Columbine, Jonesboro, fruit of rebellion.

A local weekly newspaper revealed the goals of the "kiddies lib" movement, as they published a five-part, front-page series of articles dealing with children's liberation. The first article was titled, "Prisoners of Childhood."

Their approach was that the youth of our nation represent an *oppressed minority* and that *"our laws deny human rights to anyone under eighteen years of age."* In support of their allegation, they quoted John Holt in his revolutionary book, *Escape From Childhood,* in which he argues, "That being a child, being wholly subservient and dependent, does most children more harm than good. It keeps them," Holt writes, *"in effect, prisoners of childhood."*

Consequently, the local news article continues quoting Holt, *"Discrimination against youth should be abolished, and children ought to be able to do what any adult may legally do!"* That statement sounds shocking, does it not?

The author of the article continues by reporting that humanist Richard Farson has joined Holt, and a growing crowd of adults, in advocating a child's bill of rights, saying that it would be vastly more far reaching than the one created by the UN in its International Year of the Child!

Dan Croghan, our church radio engineer, returned after taking a broadcast tape to the radio station, bringing an item just off the news wire service. The engineer at the radio station said, "Take this news item to Pastor Culwell. Perhaps he can use it." The item, datelined Coopville, Washington, reported that 9-year-old Michelle McCudgeon, perhaps the nation's youngest lobbyist, with her special interest in a national children's day, had begun her campaign by writing to two presidents. She had convinced Governor Dixie Lee Ray to declare June 10th as Children's Day in Washington State.

With keen insight, Dan observed that, at the age of six when she began, she must have had a great deal of guidance and encouragement in her efforts. This item is shared at this point to illustrate how the movement is being promoted, so as to infiltrate the ranks of children, even starting at the age of six! We said that this assault is against the family. However, as such, it becomes an assault against the entire structure and fabric of our society. Consequently, continuing our search for the solution to Columbine, our emphasis is by necessity on the family, with specific concern regarding the parent-child relationship.

God's Plan

The first part of our solution has been in discovering God's plan for the parent-child relationship, emphasizing that we must get our families planted solidly on that foundation, and teach it to others.

We have considered how every child has a specific, unique design or bent, emphasizing that there are three parts to that bent—a bent from God towards good that we must discover, and cooperate with God in developing it, a bent toward evil, inherited from Adam, which we must recognize and control, and a number of specific bents or tendencies genetically inherited from parents. Note: While the child outside of Christ has inherited a sin nature, no child is innately good apart from regeneration through faith in Christ.

Our aim is to motivate parents to get to know these bents, in order to cooperate with God in producing the finished product that He desires. Here will be another facet in the solution to the Columbine malady. For this reason, we will continue dealing with the child's bent toward evil, inherited from Adam, with a brief introduction regarding specific bents inherited from parents.

The Evil Bent

Every child has inherited a sin nature from Adam. We are reminded of that truth, previously identified through a consideration of Romans, chapter 5, verse 12, where we are told that sin entered mankind through Adam and death as a result of that sin.

As we observed earlier, if parents fail to recognize Adam's bent towards evil, they will never be able to understand the conflict that rages.

While the bent of good from God must be developed, the bent of evil from Adam must be broken. One apart from the other will lead to disaster.

Recognition of the Problem

We are reminded of King David's great cry of repentance after his heinous sin in his adulterous relationship with Bathsheba and the death of her husband Uriah, which he had arranged. We have considered his words of repentance as recorded in the fifty-first Psalm, in which he said, *"Behold, I was brought forth in iniquity, and in my sin my mother conceived me."*

David, along with every person ever born, other than Christ, has a sin nature. Consider an amplified, expanded rendering of David's words, *"Behold, I was brought forth in a state of iniquity, a state of sin. My mother, who conceived me, was sinful, and I too am sinful."*

The act of conception is not a sin, as some have suggested, but rather we are being told that all are born with a sin nature, including the child's mother.

Furthermore, we are told in Ephesians, chapter 2, verse 3, that men "were by nature children of wrath." The words found in Psalm 58, verse 3 reinforce this truth, *"the wicked are estranged from the womb; They go astray as soon as they are born."* Notice, if you will, that the child is estranged from the womb, from the very beginning of life, being bent toward evil.

If the results of that nature are ignored, and one follows humanist Holt's advice, which is that "Children ought to be able to do what any adult may legally do," parents have a real problem on their hands.

Some may feel that Holt's statement sounds good on the surface, but continuing with Holt's application, he makes it clear that those rights include "the right to travel and choose an alternative home environment." In other words, Holt says that children should have the right to go wherever they want to go and to choose a new home if they do not like their present home!

You may conclude that such a possibility is far fetched, but we already have laws on the books in the state of California that essentially permit that privilege. A family in the church I pastored for twenty-eight years suffered great anguish as the result of the freedom imposed by such laws. Imagine that small children could have the right to choose a different home, if they don't like their present abode.

Another outgrowth from Holt's position is the right of the child to control one's education, and of course we are already seeing that action as students demand the privilege of running the institution they are attending. We find those views, those philosophies gaining momentum, even in our high schools. What is the answer? What will happen if this bent toward evil is ignored?

Finding the Answer

The answer to this question and corresponding problem is found in a statement made by, of all people, the Minnesota Crime Commission. The statement was made in an effort to explain the reason for crime. Just consider their statement:

*Every baby starts life as a little savage. He is com-
pletely selfish and self-centered. He wants what
he wants when he wants it, his bottle, his mother's
attention, his playmates toy, his uncle's watch. Deny
him these and he seethes with rage and aggressive-
ness, which would become murderous, were he not
helpless.*

*He is, in fact, dirty, has no morals, no knowledge,
no skills.*

*This means that all children, not just certain chil-
dren, all children are born delinquent. If permitted to continue in this self-centered world of his
infancy, given free reign to his impulsive actions to
satisfy his wants, every child would grow up to be a
criminal, thief, killer, rapist.*

Those are strong words, but isn't it amazing that there
are people who dispute biblical teaching that everyone is
born with a sin nature. The reader may fall into this category
and be inclined to resist and reject such strong language as
that of the Minnesota Crime Commission. Yet, if you turn
some of those children loose without direction and supervision, you will see just how dirty they get.

Is it any wonder that we have such events as Columbine?
With the lack of training and discipline of today, the wonder
is that there are not many more such acts of violence.

One sees children regularly who are without supervision,
with little parental control. One mother, observed just today,
was being terrorized by her babe in arms while shopping
for groceries, that kind of scene being common! Then we
see more severe manifestations of rebellion in older children, when parents have not dealt with their bent through
permissiveness.

Do we begin to see the potential of children's liberation, in which parents are encouraged to ignore that sin nature, doing so with the view that children are inherently good. Parents can never successfully train a child while ignoring the poison in the child's sin nature.

The cause of Columbine is clear, and the answer to the problem is becoming obvious!

The Solution

What is the solution to the problem?

First, there can be no lasting solution apart from the individual's spiritual transformation. Efforts of reform, through education and social programs, may help to some degree in keeping us from turning our entire society into an absolute jungle, but within itself, reform, being destined for ultimate failure, can never fully succeed.

Why this conclusion? Because, as we have repeatedly reiterated, men are by nature the children of wrath, and nature cannot be reformed. It must be transformed by a higher power. By setting the sin nature free in so-called child liberation, we find rampant perversion, violent riots when people are denied and offended, and the militancy and hate of those today who threaten to terrorize society.

The only real and sure solution is found through leading children to spiritual life, giving them the nature of Christ. This statement is made, not to discourage parents without personal faith to train their children, but to present the only perfect solution. Proper training at every level has its rewards and the potential for preventing Columbines.

Yet, in finding direction to the right solution, suppose we simply peruse the inspired words found in Paul's letter to the Ephesians, chapter 2, verses 1 through 10.

Paul points out to the Ephesians in verse one that having been dead in sin, God has given them life. The Apostle tells them in verses two and three what their tendencies have been in the past when spiritually dead, when they walked in sin according to the course of this world system, according to the devil, the prince of this world. Their lives had been lives of disobedience, pursuing the lusts of the flesh.

Paul continues his message in verses four and five, permitting the Ephesians to know that, although they had been spiritually dead in their sin and walked in lust, now God had given them life through Christ, having been saved from their sin nature.

The great Apostle continues writing in this vein, until he reaches the words found in verse ten which are so important for our consideration. It is here that we find that we *"are His workmanship, created in Christ Jesus for good works."*

The new life in Christ gives the individual the potential of being God's workmanship, dealing with the Adamic bent and enabling the individual to do "good works."

Growth is Essential

We must not stop here, for there must be a continuous growth of the new nature through training, which includes restraint of the old nature through instruction and discipline.

Discipline is absolutely essential, its nature and extent dependent on the strength of the bent toward evil. Wise words are these found in Proverbs, chapter 29, verse 15, *"the rod and rebuke give wisdom, But a child left to himself brings shame to his mother."*

Correction and discipline are in order if evil is to be brought under control. The child who demands and gets his own way brings shame to his mother, his parents. If parents bring a child into the world and ignore the Adamic nature, giving him his desires with no effort to exert control, the parents will reap shame as a result.

The Adamic bent must be broken. One is not to break the child, but break his bent toward evil.

All parents, believers or not, must recognize the potential for evil in their children, and train and discipline them so as to break that potential. Failure to do so will result in disaster in varying degrees.

The Genes at Work

As observed earlier, every child has specific bents, genetic characteristics inherited from their parents. We will touch on this subject briefly here, waiting to explore it more fully in the following chapter.

But for now, we need to consider the principle enunciated in the book of Exodus. Moses is now on Sinai, the second time to receive the Ten Commandments. Let's tune into Moses' words:

> *Now the Lord descended in the cloud and stood with him there, and proclaimed the name of the Lord. And the Lord passed before him and proclaimed, the Lord, the Lord God, merciful and gracious, long suffering and abounding in goodness and truth, keeping mercy for thousands, forgiving iniquity and transgressions and sin, by no means clearing the guilty, **visiting the iniquity of the fathers upon the children and the children's children to the third and fourth generation.** (Exodus 34:5-7, emphasis added)*

Although the emphasis in this passage of scripture is on the mercy of God, *"keeping mercy for thousands,"* yet, let us examine these particular words appearing in verse seven, *"visiting the iniquity of the fathers upon the children and the children's children to the third and fourth generation."*

91

Interestingly and significantly, the word "iniquity" that appears in this statement literally means "to bend," "to distort," or "to pervert" as found in the Hebrew original language. Thus, what we are being told is that the Lord is visiting *the bent*, the perversion of the fathers upon the children. We find this same Hebrew word being translated *"perverse"* or *"wicked"* in Proverbs, chapter 28, verse 12. What Moses is telling us is that the presence of a perverted or wicked nature is passed on from one generation to another.

However, God will be merciful and forgiving if that perverted or wicked nature is dealt with, but the guilty, those who refuse to deal with that perverted nature, that perversion or wickedness, will be passed on to succeeding generations in inherited bents.

We find a previous reference where this same truth is expressed, as God is in the midst of giving the Ten Commandments to Moses. Dealing with the commandment prohibiting idolatry, in consideration of the Hebrew's bent toward idols, God tells Moses again that this tendency towards perversion will be passed on to succeeding generations. However, since God is merciful, if they deal with that bent toward idolatry, He will forgive them (Exodus 20:4-6).

The Bible is replete with illustrations of this truth, that is, the inheritance of perversions through the parental family line. For our purpose at this point, let us consider just one of these illustrations.

Jereboam was the first king of the Northern Kingdom of the ten tribes of Israel. His reign was exceedingly wicked, and because of his perversion, and because he did not deal with his wicked nature or those perverted characteristics, we find twenty-one times during the succeeding reigns of kings, spanning a period of 200 years, that it is said of his heirs and succeeding kings that *"they did evil in the sight of the Lord, and walked in the way of Jereboam."*

The Hebrew word translated *"way"* once again means bent or characteristic, meaning that Jereboam's heirs to the throne did the same things Jereboam did. The perverted, wicked characteristics of Jereboam were passed down to his children through succeeding kings. Through the history of the ten tribes, his original perversion went unchecked.

The undealt with wicked tendencies of parents will be passed on to their children. Parents know what their weaknesses are, thus they should train and break those same bents in the lives of their children. If not, children in succeeding generations may grow more wicked than ever in those specific areas of weakness. According to this principle, we often hear such words as — "He is just like his old man, he" or "she is just like her mother, she...."

Summary

The Adamic bent must be controlled and broken, beginning with the new birth through faith in Christ as savior, then accomplished through training, discipline, and punishment. If one follows the humanist path of "children's liberation," leaving that bent unchecked, the results described by the Minnesota Crime Commission will become an active reality.

Apparently, Harris' and Klebold's bent had not been broken, being indulged with unsupervised activities, BMW automobiles, and the likes. Had they been trained and disciplined, with their bent towards evil being broken, you and I probably would have never heard the name Columbine!

Once again, there are those genetic and habitual tendencies toward evil that are passed down to the children from their parents. The drive for materialism and excessive pursuits of pleasures, fulfilling the lusts of the flesh, seems to affect almost all people of this generation. The fear is that this tendency is already deeply imbedded in the lives of the succeeding generation. It is urgent that the lessons, the solutions contained in this treatise, be applied now. If not, the Columbines of the twentieth century may become the "Hiroshimas" of the twenty-first.

Let us be dedicated to dealing with wicked tendencies of life, whether Adamic or genetic!

Chapter Eight

When Father Knows Best

The sins and failures of one generation are passed on, and even intensified, in succeeding generations. Why is this true? The answer is because the preceding one has failed and has not provided a foundation for those who follow.

It's here that we will visit Moses on Mount Sinai once again. He is there receiving the Ten Commandments for a second time, having broken the first tablets in anger.

As we observe Moses, we are told in Exodus, chapter 34, verses 6 and 7, *"And the Lord passed before him and proclaimed, 'the Lord, the Lord God, merciful and gracious, long suffering, and abounding in goodness and truth, keeping mercy for thousands, forgiving iniquity and transgressions and sin.' "*

This passage reveals that God is merciful and forgiving. However, we also find in verse seven, that He visits "iniquity of the fathers upon the children and the children's children to the third and to the fourth generation."

The word "iniquity," if you recall from the last chapter, *means to bend or to distort or pervert.* Consequently, God is saying that the bent of one generation, the perversion or distortions of the fathers are passed on to their children and to their children's children to the third and fourth generation. The principle, emerging from this statement, tells us that the bent towards evil is passed on to children of succeeding generations.

This truth holds great significance in relation to the problem under consideration, the Columbine-type manifestation of rebellion and violence. The implication is that the failure of parents is bearing bitter fruit in the lives of their children, i.e., the problem, and its solution rest in the hands of parents.

We are then caused to understand the importance of setting the proper example for our children, dealing with and breaking the past bent towards sin.

Remember, we went to great lengths in our consideration of Psalm 139, which reveals that God designs us from our conception and in our mother's womb. From that knowledge we were able to extrapolate the truth that, in God's design, we have a bent toward good, which must be developed. We also discovered that every child has a sin nature, inherited from Adam, which must be broken.

We discovered again that there is yet a third bent or tendency that the child inherits genetically from parents, which would include the two tendencies given by God and inherited from Adam. If the parents fail to develop the design of God for good, and fail to break the Adamic tendency toward sin, the children of succeeding generations will reap bitter results.

For example, when Olga Neras was born, she inherited a very rare disease called a "severe combined immune-deficiency disease." This disease left the infant defenseless against bacteria and germs. What is being illustrated is this truth, that just as Olga was defenseless against disease, so it is that every individual is born with a severe combined immune-deficiency, *spiritually speaking*, is estranged from the womb, and is defenseless against the disease of sin.

In the case of young Olga, a physician was able to perform surgery and do a bone marrow transplant, which gave her defenses against disease. Wouldn't it be nice if the same thing could take place in relation to inherited sin disease? However, there is a twofold solution illustrated in Olga's transplant. The solution for the sin problem in the life of the individual is, one, the implantation of Christ within by faith in the new birth, thus providing defenses; and then two, the proper rearing of the child by the parents, providing training, direction, and discipline, including serving as proper role models, resulting in the availability of defenses.

Consequently, let us consider the topic, *"When Father Knows Best,"* that is, knowing what is best when he leads in breaking the Adamic bent, trains to develop the design of God for good, while serving as a role model, and setting the proper example for the children.

The Principle

Once again we consider the principle involved in the lesson before us, as we emphasized briefly in the last chapter, *the perverted ways of parents are passed on to their children.*

Examples

With that truth in mind, look with me at some biblical examples that illustrate and establish this truth.

We begin with the example of Abraham, the father of the Hebrew nation, known as the friend of God. Even so, he was vulnerable to this problem.

Actually we find a tendency, a bent within Abraham toward lying, and because he did not adequately deal with that tendency, the bent was passed on to his son Isaac, and to succeeding generations. We read in Genesis, chapter 20, verse 1, *"And Abraham journeyed from there to the south, and dwelt between Kadesh and Shur, and stayed in Gerar."*

At Gerar, as we continue reading in verse two, we discover Abraham's bent toward lying, *"Now Abraham said of Sarah, his wife, 'She is my sister.' And Abimelech, king of Gerar sent and took Sarah."*

The story continues as God appears to Abimelech in a dream and warns him concerning this relationship. Later, Abimelech asks Abraham, *"How could you do this to me? Why did you lie to me?"* And Abraham, rationalizing what he had done, replied, *"Because I thought, surely the fear of God is not in this place; and they will kill me on account of my wife."*

In other words, Abraham was interested in saving his own neck, revealing a selfish concern. However, he continues in an effort to justify his action in verse twelve, saying, *"But indeed she is truly my sister. She is the daughter of my father, but not the daughter of my mother; and she became my wife."*

Abraham said to Abimelech, "Sarah is really my half sister, and I really wasn't lying." Perhaps we find here the worst kind of lie, that which we often call a "half-truth", a lie that is built on just a kernel of truth, adding deception to the lie. Was Abraham living with Sarah as a sister? No, he was living with her as his wife. Here is a sort of "religious" kind of lie, a deception, and a half-truth in which so many people indulge. Many would call his statement a "white lie," but as the late Charles Schultz would have Lucy ask in his *Peanuts* cartoon, "Lies come in colors?"

Perhaps Abraham's action would not have been quite as bad, if it had not been a continuing problem. If one looks back to Genesis, *"Now there was a famine in the land, and Abraham went down to Egypt to dwell there, for the famine was severe in the land. And it came to pass, when he was close to entering Egypt, that he said to Sarai, his wife, 'Indeed*

I know that you are a woman of beautiful countenance'"
(Gen. 12:10-13).

He was saying, "Sarai, you are a good looking dish!
When those Egyptians see you, they will want you, and
thinking you are my wife, they will take you and kill me."
So he tells her, as recorded in verse thirteen, "Please say you
are my sister, that it may be well with me for your sake, and
that I may live because of you."

"You need me, Sarai, so tell them you are my sister.
Really wife, it's for your benefit." Really? He said, *"do this
that I may live because of you."*

What conniving, deceitful lying! He not only lies, but
also is getting his wife to lie for him, saying, "It's really for
your benefit."

Here is an example of humanistic relativism, a plague
of the twentieth century. What Abraham was doing has been
called *"situation ethics."* The end justifies the means. The
commandment not to lie is made to be *relative* and not *absolute.* Lying can be justified according to the circumstances.

Meanwhile, back to Abraham's bent. Here we discover
how it is passed on to his son Isaac, for in Genesis, chapter
26 we find Isaac doing the very same thing. He had traveled
down to the land of the Philistines, where we read in verses
six through seven, *"So Isaac dwelt in Gerar. And the men of
the place asked about his wife and he said, 'She is my sister;'
for he was afraid to say 'she is my wife,' because he thought,
'lest the men of this place kill me for Rebekah, because she
is beautiful to behold.'"*

Same song, second verse, could get better, but it's getting worse. We've heard that song before. It started with
Abraham and now is continuing in the life of his son Isaac.
Isaac was concerned for his own skin, just like his dad—a
chip off the old block!

However, the story doesn't end here. Abraham's sin has
passed to the second generation, but it doesn't stop here.

Remember that Isaac and Rebekah had twin sons, Jacob and Esau. Isaac favored Esau because he was macho, a hunter, and a man of the outdoors. Not only that, Isaac liked Esau's venison!

At the same time, Rebekah favored Jacob, and knowing that Isaac was preparing to give his blessing to Esau, she prepared a dish of goat, placing the goat's skin on Jacob's arm in order that he would feel hairy just like his brother Esau, hoping to deceive Isaac.

Now that the preparations were complete, Jacob took the counterfeit dish to his blind father Isaac, telling his father, *"I am Esau, your firstborn."* (Gen. 27:19). When Isaac became suspicious because of the circumstances, having felt the counterfeit hairy hand, he said, *"The voice is Jacob's voice but the hands are the hands of Esau"* (Gen. 27:22). After blessing Jacob, Isaac asked, *"Are you really my son, Esau?"* He (Jacob) said, *"I am"* (Gen. 27:24).

The sin has now passed to the third generation, for we remember that Jacob's name means "supplanter," which reveals how Jacob would steal Esau's birthright by supplanting him through deception.

Does the problem stop here? No, but it passed to the fourth generation. Jacob would have twelve sons, and following the example of his father, he would favor his son Joseph above all of the others.

When Joseph's brothers, through envy and jealousy, would sell Joseph into slavery, we see their efforts in covering the dastardly deed with a lie. We read in Genesis, chapter 37, verses 31 through 33 how they *"took Joseph's tunic, killed a kid of the goats and dipped the tunic in blood. Then they sent the tunic of many colors, and they brought it to their father, and said, 'we have found this. Do you know whether it is your son's tunic or not?'"*

When Jacob proclaimed that the tunic belonged to Joseph, whom he thought had fallen prey to a wild beast, his sons said nothing contradicting his conclusion. In other words, they lied in their silence as well as their action. Perhaps we use silence to perpetrate a lie more than anything else.

The lies now have gone on to the fourth generation, and one would find them continuing in succeeding generations if we had the time and space to complete the story. What a perfect example of God's word to Moses on Mount Sinai, and what a lesson to us as parents.

We reap exactly what we sow in the lives of our children. Don't blame the children, and don't blame this generation, because circumstances are what they are because of parents. Parents are the ones who have fallen prey to the humanist lies of relativity and permissiveness and have "liberated" the children to the point that they can justify almost anything.

They try to blame the schools; they try to blame the politicians and government, and they do carry a burden of guilt. However, the truth of the matter is that parents have abdicated their responsibility, and whatever has happened the parents have permitted. When the humanists and their socialist cousins succeed in kiddies' lib, don't blame them. Parents will be the ones who have permitted it, a failure leading to the Columbines of the day.

Another Example

Let us not take just one insulated example, although so big and profound. It will be fitting to examine briefly the example of King David. Abraham, the father of the Hebrew race would fail, and now we see the failure of David, the greatest of all kings, known as a man "after God's own heart."

Yet, we see a bent towards evil in the life of David, having an eye for the girls, a bent that went unchecked in his life. There was a lust in his life, when stoked by the sight of Bathsheba, sprang into a raging fire.

We see now how this bent was passed on to his children. Amnon forces his own sister Tamar, while Absalom, in his rebellion, would take the wives of David on the rooftop, in view of the entire city.

Next we look further to Solomon, who outside of Jesus, was reputedly the wisest man ever to live, seemingly wise in every area but this one inherited from his father, being the offspring of David's affair with his mother, Bathsheba.

Solomon should have known better, and yet he came to have 700 wives and 300 concubines. We read the results of his folly, this bent to sin, in 1 Kings, chapter 11, verses 1 and 3, *"But King Solomon loved many foreign women, as well as the daughters of Pharaoh: women of the Moabites, Ammonites, Edomites, Sidonians, and Hittites, and he had seven hundred wives, princesses and three hundred concubines and his wives turned away his heart"*.

We detect our principle again: when the bent of sin is established, and is not adequately curbed and corrected, it is passed on to the children and the children's children. Parents must deal with sin in their own lives and families, if they expect their children to excel.

When Father Knows Best

Consider three things that can be expected *"When Father Knows Best."* One, he will *cultivate* God's bent for good, and *correct* the Adamic bent toward evil, scrupulously following God's directions in training and setting God's plan free in their lives—true liberation!

Here is step one in children's *spiritual* liberation—and that is, dads and moms are to study the lives of their children, getting to know them personally in order to develop God's plan in their lives.

In 1934, Lazar Caplan, then the patriarch of Drummond Cutters, was handed his greatest challenge and triumph, when he was given the Yonker diamond to cut. The huge stone weighed 726 carats when it was discovered in South Africa. Ultimately Caplan would turn that great stone into twelve emerald cut gems, ranging in weight from 5.3 to 125.35 carats. Mr. Caplan would recall, "It took me two years. I spent one year just studying it, planning the size, weight, and shape of the stones." He added, "You have to understand the stone. When you don't know a stone, cleaving it can shatter it."

And so it is, parents must study and know the child's bent, the design that God has for the child, if they are to train them properly and succeed fully. Otherwise, the life is shattered.

Two, father (and mother) know best by recognizing that their children have a sin nature and a bent toward evil.

The only lasting solution to that problem comes through the new birth. So, fathers and mothers, the first priority is to lead your child to a personal, saving relationship with Christ—even before you teach him to play ball!

Three, the father (parent) who knows best will find the solution by recognizing that the children have inherited characteristics from their parents, and even from granddad and grandmother!

For example, I have some bents in my own life, believe it or not! Now, I'm not planning to confess my sins to you, but merely cite some characteristics.

I have a reputation for being very careful with my money, what little I have, and don't tell my daughter Shirley I said so, but she is very careful with her money, too. In fact, Shirley squeezes George so hard that she gives him a case of apoplexy.

On the other hand, my wife Jeanie spends and gives money so freely and is generous almost to a fault that she never has George long enough to get acquainted with him. Andrew, our youngest son, follows his mother's bent, never seeing George because he is spent before payday.

I like to dress and be as neat as possible, trying to look sharp in my clothing. Daughter Janet and Andrew have that bent. My wife likes to dress casually, followed in this bent by our son Chris.

I approach issues with strict logic and reason, followed by my daughter Shirley. My dear wife approaches matters casually and emotionally, a tendency continued by son Chris.

One hears statements such as, "He is just like his daddy; she is just like her mother."

These are very simple examples, but never minimize the potential influence you will have on your children, and even your children's children to the third and fourth generation.

We can never over emphasize the importance of parental influence. Charles Manson, a mass murderer came from a 14-year-old prostitute who walked the street. On the other hand, the offspring of the great Jonathan Edwards read like a Who's Who, made up of preachers, judges, lawyers, teachers, and professors, a multitude of professional and successful people of quality.

You see, those specific bents can just as well be good and positive, as well as negative and evil.

Summary

When father (parent) knows best, he will first do everything possible to lead his children to Christ. Two, he will do everything possible to know all about the character of his children, so as to minister to their character needs, meaning that he will study diligently to know them. Three, he will do everything possible to be consistent in proper correction and discipline, exercising leadership in every area of life. Four, he will do everything possible in being consistent and dependable, setting a proper example, being a good role model, teaching values to his children, and making spiritual values a priority.

Ephesians, chapter 6, verse 4 tells us "*not to provoke our children to wrath, but to bring them up in the nurture and admonition of the Lord.*"

We read in Proverbs, chapter 20, verse 7 that "*the just man walks in integrity,*" meaning he sets a good example for his children. When he does, his children are blessed as they follow him.

A news release serves as an illustration with which we conclude this chapter, the news release said, "*A survey of Who's Who among American high school students finds that* **the nation's outstanding teenagers are keen on religion, and maintain traditional moral values. Ninety-two percent of student leaders believe there is a personal God or vital force** *in the world. Ninety percent say that religion plays a significant role in their moral standards, 81 percent belong to an organized religion and 62 percent attend services weekly.*"

Those are the spiritual qualifications of the outstanding teenage leaders.

A solution to Columbine!

Chapter Nine

The Greatest of These

July 22, 1999 was a beautiful spring-like day in the Sierra Mountains of California, a time when you could revel in the majesty of Yosemite National Park.

Yet, in the midst of such an idyllic setting came the shocking news that the headless body of Joie Ruth Armstrong, an attractive 26-year-old naturalist, had been found in the woods, her head later located near her body.

This grisly news flashed across Northern California, announcing that the FBI and local authorities were searching for information that would lead them to the perpetrator of this macabre crime.

Just two days later, 37-year-old Cary Stayner, described as a "likable motel handyman," was arrested at a nudist colony fifteen miles southeast of Sacramento and charged with the grisly murder. It was reported that he had confessed to the murder of Armstrong, telling how after decapitating Armstrong with a knife, "Her body was left half-submerged in a nearby stream, then her head was tossed in a deeper spring-fed pool."

A brief time later it would be reported that he had also confessed to the murder of three others in February: 42-year-old Carole Sund, 15-year-old Julie Sund, and 16-year-old Silvina Pelosso. Reportedly he had strangled Carole and Silvina at the motel where he worked, thrusting their bodies into the trunk of their rented car. Then driving to a secluded area, he reportedly dragged "Julie to a secluded spot on a nearby hillside, where he cut her throat so severely he almost severed her head."

"Stayner had been fantasizing about killing women for thirty years," from the age of seven, reported the *San Jose Mercury News*. The report described "his first dark vision" as, at the age of seven, he sat in the family car outside a grocery store in his hometown of Merced and fantasized about killing the checkout girls working in the store.

How could a human being commit such crimes against innocent women? Friends and family members, when informed replied, "the Cary we all knew is not capable of these crimes."

Could this tragedy have been avoided? Why was this 7-year-old quiet, handsome boy not able to discuss his problem with his parents, and deal with this aberrant problem?

We can only speculate as to the answer. However, news accounts give strong hints as we are told that he had a distant, fearful relationship with a stern mother, words that would indicate that there had been little if any communication regarding his problems with her.

Furthermore, his father who "provided the hugs," evidently became obsessed over the abduction of Steven, a younger son. It is possible that this obsession would alienate Cary, leading to neglect. The newspaper reported that "the family withdrew after Delbert [Cary's father] spent evenings in Steven's dark room, lying on his bed and smelling his clothes." Years later, when Cary had painted over Steven's name in the garage, "his father rushed in and stopped him. In a rage, Delbert wiped off the fresh paint as quickly as he could."

Various incidents were reported which manifested problems in Cary's life, including the use of marijuana. Yet his father would say, "If he had problems, he sure never told anybody. He was a quiet boy."

If, and this is a big IF, if Cary would have had a warm, loving relationship with his mother, would he have confided in her and found help? Boys do discuss problems with loving mothers, and confide in them. My sons, plus half of the kids in church, confided with my wife, dealing with the most sensitive areas of life.

In addition, suppose the father had been more attentive, loving, and less obsessed with the loss of his other son, would there have been the potential that Cary would have confided in him, thus dealing with his aberrant problem?

We can only speculate. However, it is true, as Sharon Pagaling, chief criminal profiler for the California Department of Justice, said, *"the research on serial killers shows they have a common failure to bond with parental figures, a lack of intimate, emotional relationships with other people."*[1]

Why have I spent so much time dealing with this extreme account? Simply to illustrate the importance of a loving bond between parents and their children! As we find in 1 Corinthians, chapter 13, verse 13, *"Now abides faith, hope, love, these three, but the greatest of these is love."*

We can train, know, and discipline our children, but all will be to no avail apart from a bond of love. We have speculated regarding Cary Stayner, but one thing of which I am sure, training, knowing, and disciplining in the *bond of love* can prevent the warping of a child's life, even a Cary Stayner!

Remember Harris and Klebold of Columbine? BMWs would not solve their problem, but what if there had been a deeper bond of love? It seems that manifestations of their problems were obvious, but for some reason, love didn't step in to prevent death from going to school!

A friend of Eric Harris said that Harris' father discovered a pipe bomb in his son's bedroom in the months before the Columbine massacre. Nate Dykman said in a *Good Morning America* interview that Harris told him his parents disposed of the bomb themselves and didn't report it to authorities because he was in a juvenile-diversion program for another matter.[2]

What does this parental response have to say about the relationship between parents and son? We must be careful not to read too much between the lines, yet there seems to be an absence of real love in action. Perhaps love would have found a way, even at this late date, to avoid the eventuality of the Columbine tragedy.

In light of what has been written, isn't it interesting to note that the secular humanists, and all of their cousins in Women's and Children's Liberation, have ignored the ingredient of love. The consequences have resulted in a fragmentation and destruction of the family unit.

Efforts are made to turn control of the children over to childcare centers and the schools. In supposedly "freeing" mom, they have destroyed the "love center" of the home. Mom is now so busy making a career outside the home, that in so many cases, the *"love career"* on the inside has been sacrificed and lost.

Even secular authorities recognize there is no substitute for the parent (mother)-child relationship. An article from the Associated Press, written by Wendy Dreskin, under the headline, "Growing Concern About Effects of Daycare on Kids," observed,

> *Many child psychologists, educators, pediatricians and even parents are becoming increasingly concerned about the effects of daycare on the child. A child's capacity to love is formed in the first two years of life. The key is what psychologists call bonding, a lasting, mutual attachment between the*

*child and a loving adult, **usually the mother. If this
is missing it may affect his ability to develop future
human relationships.***[3] **(emphasis added)**

The author would add later, *"When children are raised
away from parental love there can be a retardation of
development."*

She continues by quoting Dr. Phyllis Levenstein, professor at State University in New York at Stonybrook, *"Where
there is no human attachment, [by that they mean the bonding
relationship of love] there can be no conscience, adults denied
bonding form a large part of the criminal population."* [4]

When will leaders, educators, and politicians learn that
they cannot solve the "Columbine" and other related problems through education or legislation? More money, smaller
class size, finer facilities, and teachers can never do what
only parents can do!

For that reason, we need to learn more about establishing
the love relationship in the home.

A Progressive Development

Let us consider some truths from Psalm 127 and 128,
where we find the *beginning*, the *building*, the *broadening*,
and the *blessing* of the family relationship.

The Beginning

There can be no other place to begin than the husband-
wife relationship. Suppose we consider Psalm 127, verses 1
and 2, *"Unless the Lord builds the house, they labor in vain
who build it: unless the Lord guards the city, the watchman
stays awake in vain. It is vain for you to rise up early, to
sit up late, to eat the bread of sorrows: for He gives His
beloved sleep."*

Significantly, that word translated "house" is used in different ways. Sometimes it means just a house, like the one in which we live. In other cases it refers to the *household* or literally to the *family*.

For example, we find this same word appearing in Genesis, chapter 7, verse 1, where God tells Noah, "Come into the ark, you and all your household." The same word is used here that is translated house in Psalm 127, verse 1. Obviously God wasn't instructing Noah to dismantle his house and bring the roof, the rafters, the walls, and the floors into the ark. No, God was saying, bring your "household," your family—your wife, your three sons, and their wives into the ark.

Laying the Foundation

Get the picture? We are being told that, unless the husband and wife depend on the Lord in building their relationship and laying the foundation for the family, all of their labor will be in vain.

The comparison of the husband-wife relationship and the building of the family foundation with that of a city is interesting. In this comparison the Psalmist says, unless the Lord guards the city, the watchman wastes his time in staying awake!

We see that it makes no difference how big the wall or how strong the fortifications of a city may be, or how careful and diligent the watchman is, unless it is done by the power and under the leadership of God, it will be for naught.

Reading this we think about the ancient city of Babylon. Ancient historians tell us that the city walls were built to be impregnable. The walls were so great that three or four chariots could supposedly run side by side along the top of the wall, the height being similarly great. Yet, in spite of those defenses, the Medes and Persians could march into the city and conquer it without entering into battle.

No city is invulnerable unless God sets a watch over it. Our emphasis here is, unless the Lord builds the family and is permitted to set His guard about it, the family becomes vulnerable and faces failure. The home must be founded on the leadership and love of God, and the place to begin is with the foundation, as any wise builder would know, the husband and wife forming that foundation.

The family circle is never complete apart from the inclusion of our Father God. Paul recognizes this truth as he writes in Ephesians, chapter 5, verse 21 that husbands and wives are to submit to one another *in the fear of God*. God's plans for a marriage are incomplete apart from His leadership and the husband's and wife's reverence, respect, and submission to Him.

When does a couple begin building the foundation for marriage and ultimately the family? They begin long before even getting married, during dating and courtship. If that building period includes carelessness and promiscuity, indelible scars, including distrust, disrespect, and insecurity may result.

A man and woman abandoning purity build upon sand. Consider the example of Amnon and Tamar, children of King David, who were half brother and sister.

We are told that, *"Absalom the son of David had a lovely sister, whose name was Tamar; and Amnon the son of David loved her"* (2 Sam. 13:1). The name Tamar literally means *"palm tree,"* giving indication of her stately beauty. We would say today that she was a "real dish."

We continue reading in the next verse that, *"Amnon was so distressed over his sister Tamar that he became sick."* Amnon was lovesick over this beautiful half-sister. The verse continues by telling us that, *"she was a virgin and it was improper for Amnon to do anything to her"* (2 Sam. 13:2).

Apparently because they were half-sister and brother, Amnon could have married her. In the face of Amnon's

113

advances, Tamar pleaded with him, *"Do not do this disrespectful thing! Please ask the King, for he will not withhold me from you"* (2 Sam. 13:12, 13).

But because Amnon was so consumed by his lustful desire, "he forced her" (verse 14). The lesson for which we search is found in the results of Amnon's foolish actions. We read in verse fifteen, *"Then Amnon hated her exceedingly, so that his hatred with which he hated her was greater than the love with which he had loved her. And Amnon said to her, 'Arise and be gone!'"*

We understand that this example is extreme, and yet it reveals to us that it is not unusual to find guilt, jealousy, distrust, and disrespect blighting marital happiness where there has been impure action in courtship.

How is it that men and women insist on building family relationships when the relationships are not honoring to God? Yet, multitudes today are just like Amnon, seeking self-gratification for the moment, failing to consider long-term consequences.

Parents fail to model and teach purity, and schools teach sex-education without standards and provide condoms! How desperately we need to rediscover and emphasize how to begin by laying a proper foundation.

The Building

After beginning properly with the husband-wife relationship, let us go on to consider *building* the family with the parent-child relationship.

We turn to Psalm 127 once again, this time considering verses 3 through 5,

> *"Behold, children are a heritage from the Lord,*
> *the fruit of the womb is a reward.*
> *Like arrows in the hand of a warrior,*

So are the children of one's youth.
Happy is the man who has his quiver full of them;
They shall not be ashamed,
But shall speak with their enemies in the gate."

A step-by-step consideration of these inspired words will be helpful and enlightening.

The Psalmist begins by emphasizing that "children are a *heritage* from the Lord." The Hebrew word translated *"heritage"* literally means "a *possession" or "a property."* The verb form carries the thought of giving an assignment. Putting these thoughts together, it is discovered that children are God's possession, God's property, and are given as an assignment to parents!

The Parent's Assignment

Parents have the responsibility of discovering God's design of His children, God's bent for their lives, including this assignment to complete the job begun by the Lord.

What a beautiful concept—that children are the possession of God and that God has given them as an assignment to their earthly parents. The last phrase of verse three reinforces this figure as we are told, *"the fruit of the womb is a reward."*

Children do not come to us simply as a result of a biological process, but as God's possession given to parents as "a reward."

Now, if children are a gift to their parents, looking at the other side of this truth, we would conclude that, in a very real sense, parents are a gift to their children.

Considering these aspects of the parent-child relationship that both children and parents are gifts from God, we conclude that God never makes a mistake. There may times when parents think, "Why aren't my children more like George's and Helen's?" Children sometimes ask, "Why aren't my parents like Josephine's?"

The answer is that God specially designs both for each other! Both simply need to fulfill their assignments with that which God has given.

Children to be Directed by Parents

Children are *"like arrows in the hand of a warrior,"* we are told in verse four. That imagery tells us that children are to be under the control and direction of their parents. Just as a warrior very carefully determines the goal or target at which he will shoot, carefully aiming his arrow, so parents have the responsibility of directing or aiming their children's lives.

The target or goal is the design that God has set for them. Remember that we are told to "train up a child in the way he should go," according to his God given bent or design. Parents are not to just permissively permit their children to do their own thing, hoping that in some way or another they will accidentally come out all right.

Such a philosophy is of the secular world and comes from such men as John Dewey, signer and allegedly author of the *Humanist Manifesto,* also known as the father of modern education. Dewey, his fellow humanists, and modern day fellow travelers have blighted our youth and educational system with the doctrine of *"relativism,"* in which we are told there is no absolute truth. Dewey would say in 1927, that "it was wrong to believe in something that could not change."

Dewey's views, which dominate the public educational system, since he is known as the father of modern progressive education, clearly reveal that our public educational system cannot fulfill the role that we are considering.

As far as Dewy was concerned, all morals, standards of right and wrong, are relative, there being no absolutes. Consider these selected views held by and propounded by Dewey.

Concerning the validity of absolute principles, Dewey would write that principles are relative and are manifested in *"a man who insists upon having his own way without learning from experience what is the better way. He fancies that some abstract principle justifies his course of action without recognizing that his principle needs justification—appeal to principle is either purely verbal, or a form of obstinate pride,"* Dewey insists. *(emphasis* added).

Concerning morals, Dewey would again insist that there are no absolute standards of morality, but that all are relative, depending on circumstances. He would write, *"To attempt to get similar results from lessons about morals in a democratic society is to rely upon sentimental magic."* Furthermore Dewey would write, *"all, which we have been criticizing and which the idea of education sets forth, spring from taking morals too narrowly, giving them, on one side, a sentimental goody-goody turn without reference to effective ability to do what is socially needed, on the other side, overemphasizing convention so as to limit morals to a list of definitely stated acts. As a matter of fact, morals are as broad as acts which concern our relationship with others"*[5] (emphasis added).

Since the teachings of Dewey, morals and values form the foundation of modern education, which holds that morals or values cannot be taught. We would then conclude that under these views, since all morals are relative, that if they are taught they will represent only the views of the teacher for that moment in time and the prevailing circumstances.

The eighteenth century philosopher, Jean Jacques Rousseau said, in a quote universally known, *"Man is born free, but now is everywhere in chains."* Rousseau's idea was that man is naturally good and pure, but that society has made him evil and twisted. Consequently, the view is that we should return to a kind of education that would permit children to run free, without any inhibitions that were traditionally instilled in them. Since these ideas have so greatly influenced professional educators, as those seen in the views of Dewey that are being propounded in the halls of academia, it is obvious why there has been such a dramatic increase in violence in our schools.

Obviously, the public educational system cannot fulfill parental duties under consideration and is ill equipped to deal with problems that depend on morality, no matter how elaborate the system becomes or how much money is invested in it.

Such teaching should not deceive parents, but as a warrior they must have an absolute purpose in view. Warriors don't just "shoot an arrow into the air," not knowing or caring where it will fall, but takes careful aim.

So parents are to aim the lives of their children carefully toward God's goal for them. Any other way is like what I call the "Burger King Philosophy, Have it your way," that is, any old way will do. That philosophy may go well with hamburgers, but such permissiveness will lead children to ruin.

A Difficult Task

We may be sure that God selected the figure of an arrow carefully, because the shooting of an arrow is very difficult to master with accuracy. I recall traveling with my wife to visit her brother, then living in San Francisco. Roald, her brother, and a neighbor were into archery. While visiting one day, the two of them were practicing shooting at a target on a bale of hay in a vacant lot.

As I watched, I thought I could hit that bale of hay with my eyes closed. After watching them for awhile, Roald handed the bow and an arrow to me, asking if I would like to shoot.

First of all, I could hardly pull the bow. When I finally succeeded, letting the arrow go, it hit about halfway to the bale of hay. I was humiliated! So I haven't tried to shoot too many arrows since then, but I want to tell you that the act of accurately shooting an arrow is difficult to master.

Thus, we find that this figure chosen by God was not mere happenstance, for directing the life of a child is difficult. Nurturing, directing, tending, and cultivating the lives of children will require real commitment, effort, and determination.

In addition, parents are responsible for giving children direction and protection outside of the home as well as on the inside. The Bible speaks of building a hedge about them for protection. Such a view has given rise to the accusation that to do so is like rearing them in a "hot-house." Thus, we are told that, when they grow up after being in this hot house environment, they will not know how to cope with the things of the world. Such a position is just like saying, throw your children in the garbage can so they will know about garbage, and then they will know how to deal with garbage.

Direction also involves *protection*. The old excuse, I'm not going to tell my children what to do, but let them grow up and make their own choice, is an irresponsible abdication of parental responsibility. The parents of John Walker of Marin County, California took this precise approach in rearing their son, resulting in his journey to Afghanistan to become a Taliban fighter, leading to treasonous charges and probable imprisonment! Such can be the sad results when parents fail in directing the lives of their children.

The Broadening

As we consider *the broadening* of this relationship we are reminded that, when you shoot an arrow, you don't grip it tightly with your fist. What will happen if you have the shaft of the arrow in a tight grip? One thing for sure—you will not hit the target.

The point here is that so many parents smother their children, keeping them in such a tight grip that they never learn responsibility. We are not suggesting that parents just turn children loose and permit them to do their own thing, but after giving them direction, give them freedom to do what is right and to learn how to function responsibly. Such freedom may lead to failure, but children can learn through failure when properly managed.

God gives his children freedom to fail, which often results in some of the best lessons of life. While training our children, we must do the same.

The purpose in aiming an arrow is letting it go, in order to hit the target. Parents aim, direct the lives of their children for that same purpose—to let them go so as to live responsibly. Parents direct their children with the goal of one-day setting them free, free to live responsibly, exercising God's design for their lives.

Think About It

God gives His children as possessions to parents as rewards, with the assignment of training and directing them to measure up to God's design.

There must be a loving relationship if parents are to succeed. Selma Fryberg, professor of child psychoanalysis at the University of Michigan wrote, *"A day care center cannot provide this relationship so essential to the child's intellectual and emotional development. Our children, and parents too, have a desperate need for an intense relationship of love, and that responsibility cannot be delegated to someone else."*[6]

The need for mothers to fulfill their family role is desperate. Mothers should see the family role as a priority. This statement was not meant to exempt fathers. However, it is the loving role of the mother that is being lost, as wives/

mothers fall prey to the feminist philosophy pervading the land, thrusting them into business and professional careers.

So many children are languishing for parental love. Just providing food, fun, shelter, and clothing is not enough.

The Blessing

Every duty or responsibility given by God, when fulfilled brings *blessings*. Here we are drawn to Psalm 128, verse 1 through 3:

> *Blessed is every one who fears the Lord,*
> *Who walks in His ways.*
> *When you eat the labor of your hands,*
> *You shall be happy,*
> *and it shall be well with you.*
> *Your wife shall be like a*
> *fruitful vine*
> *In the very heart of your house,*
> *Your children like olive plants*
> *all around your table.*

Blessed, happy is *everyone* who fears the Lord and who *walks* in His ways. Notice the word *walks,* which indicates that He has in mind a continuing relationship. The process goes on and on, and as it does, "You shall be happy, and it shall be well with you." The training continues as parents "walk in His ways."

Go back and read verse three again, finding the results, the blessings of that steadfast walk. What a graphic, picturesque, vivid, beautiful portrait we find there of the loving, happy family.

Mother

The wife/mother *"shall be like a fruitful vine."* Only a farmer can fully appreciate the image described here. Nothing delights him more than the sight of a vine laden with fruit, or a similarly productive tree.

Such terminology is not meant to suggest that such fruitfulness involves only giving birth to children, but includes the finished product as well—the conception, birth, and maturity of the fruit—the complete finished product of the training process.

Notice the place the wife/mother holds in the family, "in the very *heart* of your house (household, family)." She is at the center, thus the very heart and heartbeat of the family. The family simply cannot function properly apart from the lifeblood of love she produces!

Children

If the wife is "like a fruitful vine," what fruit does she bear? The answer— *"children like olive plants all around your table."*

One, we see children, not only just as fruit, but as plants well-prepared, trained, directed, ready to bear fruit also. Parents can know no greater joy or blessings than in seeing their children mature into healthy, profitable productive "plants."

As I think of my own children, they bring a great delight to my heart. Faithful, committed, mature, fruitful, wholesome, moral, spiritual, dedicated, all words descriptive of my two girls and three boys, and even some foster children too! I see other parents who are similarly blessed, but at the same time I see many who grieve over their children because they have not matured "like olive plants."

Two, I observe the joy of fellowship as the children are pictured as being "all around your table." There is no other fellowship to compare with that which is enjoyed around the table at mealtime. This truth is implied in the words of our Savior as He promises, *"Behold, I stand at the door and knock. If anyone hears my voice and opens the door, I will come in to him and dine with him, and he with me"* (Rev. 3:20).

Here is a place where love is *shared* at its best. Parents should find a lesson in the words found here. Families are so fragmented often because they fail to sit down and eat together regularly. There is no other place where sharing, at its most meaningful level, takes place where, in this informal familiar setting, children and parents open their hearts and share in a loving nonthreatening manner. Meal times should be sacred family time, carefully guarded and cultivated.

Father

The presence of fathers is included in these words found in Psalm 128, *"Your wife, Your children."*

The father is admonished, *"And you, fathers, do not provoke your children to wrath, but bring them up in the training and admonition of the Lord"* (Ephesians 6:4).

That word translated *"training,"* in the NKJV is translated *"nurture"* in the authorized version (KJV).

Just visualize the scene that word brings to mind when coupled with the scene depicted in Psalm 128. Here you fathers are sitting around your table. There is also your wife like a fruitful luscious vine, with all of your children like tender olive plants surrounding you. Your responsibility is to *nurture, train, and cultivate* those tender plants in order that they grow and also become fruitful.

Do you suppose that we have visualized here a "family classroom," where children are being trained and bonds of love are being developed? Fathers are listening to the children, not in indifference, but in loving interest. They respond with gentle instruction, conversing lovingly, giving wise direction toward proper goals.

In an article entitled, "Study: Dad's Key to Solving Drug Use," we find an illustration of the importance of the role of the father under consideration here. Consider some words from this secular news release:

> *Ok dads, listen up. The key to winning the war on drugs rests not with the police or laws, but with you.*
>
> *A national survey released Monday shows that dads who eat dinner with their children, take them to religious services and help them with homework, greatly reduce the chances their kids will smoke, drink or use illegal drugs. "We need a return of the family dinner in America," said Joseph Califano, Jr., president of the National Center on Addiction and Substance Abuse at Columbia University, which conducted the study.*

The news article continued:

> *The trouble is that most kids don't think they can turn to their dads for advice about drugs. Nearly 60 percent of the teens surveyed said their mothers are easier to talk to about drugs. Only 26 percent said the same about their dads.*

What an indictment on today's dads!

Yet, what a happy scene we find depicted in Psalm 128. Parents, are you doing it? God richly rewards those who fulfill this responsibility in their God-assigned roles.

On the other hand, our dear heavenly Father will hold parents responsible for neglecting this relationship. He will not hold the school responsible. He will not hold the state responsible. He will not hold the childcare centers responsible. Why? God has not given the responsibility to these NGO's, but to parents.

He has given the children, who are His possessions, into the hands of parents, giving them the assignment to determine His design for their lives and train them accordingly.

This assignment is given to both parents, and when they fail to any degree, severe are the consequences, as illustrated in the news article previously cited. The same study just referenced illustrates, in one area, just how important the two-parent model is:

The latest statistics on teenage drug use, gathered in the survey, show how far parents have to go:

About 14 million youngsters 12 to 17 are at moderate to high risk of using illegal substances, based on their habits and relationships.

Children in two-parent homes who don't get along with their fathers are 68 percent more likely to try illegal drugs than teens in supportive two-parent homes.

Kids raised by single mothers are 30 percent higher risk than in supportive two-parent homes.

The words of a poet rattle about in my brain, that roughly say as I recall, *"I've walked the world over in my search for teachers true, and from the throngs that crowd life's lanes, I have selected you"* (with apologies; author unknown).

No plan is complete if not permeated with love, for "the greatest of these is love."

Notes

1. *San Jose Mercury News*, 22 July-2 August 1999.

2. *The Denver Post*, 28 May 1999.

3. Wendy Dreskin, *Santa Cruz Sentinel*, 17 June 1979.

4. Ibid.

5. John Dewey, *Democracy and Education*, Chapter 26, 1916.

6. *Santa Cruz Sentinel*, 17 June 1979.

7. *San Jose Mercury News*, 31 August 1999.

Chapter Ten

The Rod of Love
Part One

" *Spare the rod and spoil the child"* is a very familiar statement, which on the surface may sound rather harsh. However, a much stronger statement is found in Proverbs, chapter 24 where we are told, *"He who spares his rod hates his son."*

We have previously discussed how to build the love relationship between parents and children within the family unit. There is a mistaken view abroad that if parents discipline or punish their children, they must not love them. There are those who feel that parents cannot possibly love their children while subjecting them to pain. Yet, as we will find, real love must include discipline.

The result of prevailing permissive views has led to a drought of meaningful discipline and has produced and almost semi-state of anarchy among some youth. Thus, it is essential that we learn that there has never been order apart from discipline, even in the animal world.

Its lack, beginning in the family, continuing through the

school and reaching to the highest levels of society, has been a major contributing factor to the problem under consideration. Consider the following account that so graphically illustrates the level to which discipline has declined, as the state has intruded into family life.

On Monday, 13 September 1999, Donald Cobble sat watching his lawyer defend him before the Massachusetts Supreme Court against allegations that he was a child abuser.

Cobble, associate pastor of a nondenominational church in Woburn, Massachusetts, had openly acknowledged that he had done precisely what he was accused of doing—punishing his 12-year-old son Judah by spanking him with a belt.

Young Judah, when 9-years-old, had brought home a report from his teacher, bearing two "x's," indicating bad behavior. When Judah gave his father the note, Dad said, "Okay, you're going to get *two licks* with the belt because you got two x's."

These "licks" consisted of two whacks on Judah's clothed bottom with the soft end of a belt, leaving "pink marks on his body" that would fade after ten minutes. According to his belief in the teaching of Scripture, dad Cobble had given Judah a spanking, and not much of a spanking at that.

When Judah was faced with another bad report, he pleaded with the teacher, "No, don't do that, he'll spank me again." The bureaucratic wheels were set in motion. The teacher and a "behavioral management specialist" interrogated Judah about his father's disciplinary methods. After a meeting with the parents, the teacher, the principal, and the "specialist," a report was filed with the Massachusetts Department of Social Services, a report recommending that the department investigate possible abuses.

After a representative of the department, a state social worker, interviewed Judah and his parents, she filed a report supporting the claim that Mr. Cobble had physically abused his son. She also cited Mrs. Cobble for "neglect" because she did not prevent her husband from spanking their child! Another social worker continued the investigation later and presented Mr. Cobble with a "service plan." The plan specified that he was to acknowledge the harmful effects of physical abuse on his son, "acknowledge responsibility for abusing Judah," "refrain from using further physical discipline and attend individual therapy as a means of learning new, more appropriate ways of disciplining Judah."

When Cobble refused to sign the service plan, the state took no further action. However, Cobble, being branded as a "child abuser," set out to clear his name. He first challenged the findings in an administrative hearing of the Social Services Department, in which the department insisted their report was accurate, meaning that Cobble was in reality, a "child abuser."

When he filed a lawsuit against the department, Superior Court Judge John Cratsley ruled against him. When Mr. Cobble appealed, the Supreme Judicial Court chose to take the case, directly bypassing the appellate court. At the date of this writing, the author knows of no decision.

We learn, through such actions as this, that the state has usurped the parental right to punish children for wrongdoing. In fact, the state prohibits parents, as well as school teachers and administrators, from administering meaningful punishment that produces pain.

As far back as 1979, the Swedish Parliament enacted a law that stipulated that, beginning July 1 of that year, *"Parents may not strike their children or treat them in other humiliating ways."*[1] The actual wording of the law prohibits *"any act which, for the purpose of punishing, causes the child physical injury or pain, even if the disturbance is mild and passing,"* wording that is meant to include both verbal or psychological punishment.

This legislation was rather shocking in the U.S. twenty

years ago, but has become the norm twenty years later. Much earlier, corporal punishment had been abolished in the public schools. The teachings of John Dewey, known as the father of modern education, had now become the norm. Dewey wrote, *"Moral education in school is practically hopeless when we set up the development of character."*[2]

Doctor Benjamin Spock gave further credence to the elimination of corporal punishment in his writings as he contended that spanking rarely worked and advocated a loving reasonableness toward children, not the "traditional mix of punishment and fear."[3]

The *Seattle Times* quoted pediatrician Dr. Kathy Mikesell, who collaborated on the last two editions of Dr. Spock's book, saying, *"He became more and more convinced that corporal punishment was not in a child's best interest in general."*[4]

Parents must realize now that, when they apply the "board of education to the seat of knowledge," no matter how gently it is applied, they are guilty of child abuse in the eyes of the humanist and are judged so in the view of the state. One member of a children's rights organization and author of a book wrote, "the Swedish law is long overdue because so called spanking has in effect been a legalized milder form of assault and battery."

A teacher or school administrator, who dares touch a student, is open to legal civil action and possible criminal action. The humanist, secularist, and Year of the Child advocates have won the day with their so-called "children's rights," virtually eliminating punishment that produces pain at all levels.

A local, weekly news publication argued that a 6-year-old child "should be able to choose who they want to live with," with a part of that choice being based on punishment, of course. Can you just imagine a 6-year-old being able to choose with whom they want to live? It is difficult to imagine the extremes to which these advocates of permissiveness can go!

Consider the ruling of the Supreme Court of the United States of America in striking down a Massachusetts law that required parental consent for an abortion for a teenage girl. The court ruling said in part, *"We conclude that, under state regulations such as that undertaken by Massachusetts, every minor must have the opportunity, if she so desires, to go directly to court without first consulting her parents."*

Outside of the argument against abortion, what does that ruling imply? By implication and principle, it goes far beyond the issue of abortion. First of all, the court's ruling states that the court and state system knows what is best for our children and is assuming the right to direct their lives and assume control of them. Next, it keeps the children from parental control. The operator of an abortion clinic, who challenged the Massachusetts law said, "What the court is decreeing is that a personal decision of abortion is just that, a personal one and *young people are finally free,"* free from parental control and discipline. However, this freedom is rather unusual. Children are free of parental control, while at the same time are placed under the control of a permissive state!

We should know by now that we are suffering severely from an overly permissive society, in which law and order are growing more lax daily, and promiscuity and delinquency are the norm, even being legislated and condoned by the courts of our land.

In showing just how widespread the approval of such permissiveness is, I refer to "Letters to the Editor" of the *Wall Street Journal,* a letter responding to the news article about Mr. Cobble, who had dared to administer two slight blows to the gluteus maximus of his young son, punishing him for misbehavior at school. The newspaper had printed an editorial article defending Mr. Cobble's action. The attitude expressed by the letter writers could be summed up in the words of one writer from Houston, Texas. He wrote, "Three cheers for the social workers who had investigated [Donald Cobble] for child abuse." Since Cobble had based his actions on biblical teach-ings, this writer stated further that the Bible is "antiquated," further suggesting that it had been used to justify suppression of women, incest, genocide, infanticide, slavery, adultery, and segregation. Another writer cited a quote that said, "Spanking eats at the bond between parent and child."[5]

One cannot deny that corporal punishment is becoming more rare than the "spotted owl," or any number of other sup-posed threatened species. Consequently, we find how impera-tive it is that we rediscover the biblical concept and application of discipline in dealing with behavioral abuses of our day.

Our aim here is to discover just what constitutes biblical discipline, how to apply it, and to discuss briefly the results when it is not applied. The stage is set for our discovery in the inspired words of Proverbs, *"He who spares his rod hates his son, But he who loves him disciplines him promptly (or early)"* (Proverbs 13:24).

Once again we find that punishment is absolutely consis-tent with the concept of love. In fact, discipline becomes one of the highest expressions of love possible!

Two Facets

There are two facets or two sides of the coin, as it were, of biblical discipline. If one is administered apart from the other, there is an imbalance and the potential for absolute failure. We are dealing here with the breaking and curbing of the child's bent toward evil, doing so in such a manner so as not to crush the child's spirit.

Chastisement

One facet of discipline is characterized by the Hebrew word that is translated *"chastise "* or *"chastisement."* This word is the one used in the Scripture just referenced. Accurately translated, the latter part of that verse becomes clearer as it should read, *"But he who loves him chastises him early."*

That word translated "chastise" literally refers to the administration of the rod in corporal punishment, which results in pain and anguish. The Bible teaches that chastisement, resulting in pain, is essential for children. The circumstance and child involved will dictate the varying amount of pain that is essential to afflict. There are some children who are more sensitive and responsive than others. A firm word spoken to my oldest daughter had the potential of literally breaking her heart. On the other hand, a liberal application of the rod was indicated for all of my hardheaded sons.

Pain Removed

How amazing that today every effort is being made to remove any semblance of pain from what is called "punishment" in our legal system. We are told that punishment that results in pain is inhumane and must be eliminated. Different forms of capital punishment have been eliminated because of potential pain afflicted, being called "cruel and unusual punishment." Such extreme efforts made to eliminate pain, result in a "punishment" that becomes less a deterrent to crime or lawlessness.

Punishment, to be effective, must involve pain, the amount depending on the offense and the offender.

The Problem

We are told in Proverbs that *"Foolishness is bound up in the heart of a child"* (Proverbs 22:15). As we found earlier, as revealed in the Psalms, *"The wicked are estranged from the womb; They go astray as soon as they are born, speaking lies"* (Psalm 58:3).

The problem begins at birth. The word "foolish," found in Proverbs, chapter 22, verse 15 refers to one who hates instruction, one who harbors moral and spiritual decadence. *"Foolishness is bound in the heart of a child!"*

Reference was made earlier to some letters to the editor in a major newspaper, protesting a report of the gentle spanking of a child. One writer, writing in protest against such spanking, began her letter by writing, *"Spanking teaches several interesting lessons to children. It teaches them to lie."* Her premise was, fear of spanking will lead children to lie, thus, "teaching them to lie."

Have parents ever found it necessary to teach their children to lie? "Brother did it; sister caused it," "I didn't do it," such are the kinds of lies that rise unbidden to the tongues of children. We read in Psalms, chapter 58, verse 3, *"They go astray as soon as they are born, speaking lies."* Good behavior must be taught and bad behavior must be prevented, otherwise, we "sow the wind and reap the whirlwind" in the lives of our children. It isn't necessary to teach children to lie or misbehave, it comes naturally!

The Solution to the Problem

We were told in Proverbs, chapter 22, verse 15, that *"Foolishness is bound up in the heart of a child."* The solution to this problem which originates at birth, is given in reading the balance of this verse of scripture, *"the rod of correction will drive it far from him."*

The mistaken view abroad, as we have found, is that if you will just leave the child alone, when they grow up they will ultimately deal with the problem of foolishness and will get it out of their system. Not so! The Bible makes it very clear that "foolishness" must be driven out.

We find an illustration of this truth in Proverbs, chapter 14. Where we are told in verse one that *"the wise woman builds her house."*

Who is this wise woman? She is the woman who, with foolishness driven out of her life, marries and builds her household. She builds her home. She builds the family relationship, exalting that relationship.

On the other hand, we are told in that same verse, *"But the foolish [woman] pulls it down with her hands."* Who is that "foolish" woman? She is one in whom the foolishness *has not* been driven out. Thus, she plucks down the family unity; she destroys; she disrupts and tears down the family relationship.

No wonder we have a soaring divorce rate, resulting from both undisciplined permissive men and women, who have discarded biblical principles of discipline and have taken "foolishness" into marriage like a canker that destroys.

One may ask, what in the world does the failure of disciplining children have to do with the divorce rate? Simply this, when we have a generation of undisciplined people, they take that lack of discipline into the marriage and family relationship, bringing with them the potential for discord and ultimate destruction. One cannot expect an undisciplined person, who has never had foolishness expelled, to submit to a disciplined relationship.

We are challenged here to think about the marriage relationship, realizing the impact it has on the success, or the lack thereof, in the lives of the children. Marriages are doomed to failure if there is not discipline in the lives of both husband and wife. Look further to verse nine where we are told that, *"Fools mock at sin."* The meaning is clear that the individual, out of whom foolishness has not been driven, laughs at the very concept of sin and guilt. The foolish say, "Sin, what's that? Eat, drink and be merry. What's wrong with that? Have a good time." Such an attitude typifies the individual who has not been subjected to discipline.

Look further at Proverbs, chapter 19, verse 3 where we

are told, *"the foolishness of man twists [perverts] his way."* Ever wonder about the origin of perversion? It originates when foolishness has not been driven out of the life of the individual. The foolishness of man perverts his way. *"And his heart frets [rages] against the Lord."* Rebellion against God results when "foolishness" is not driven out.

Furthermore, the rod of discipline is absolutely essential in driving the foolishness from a child. Think about these inspired words from God.

"Do not withhold correction from a child, for if you beat him with a rod he will not die. You shall beat him with a rod, and deliver his soul from hell" (Proverbs 23:13-14).

If parents desire to preserve their children, they must not forsake the rod. If parents love their children and desire to deliver them from destruction, chastisement is essential.

That word "beat," as found in the passage under consideration, sounds brutal, does it not? However we are not talking about child abuse or battering, but are talking about discipline administered wisely, discipline with balance, using the rod only as needed.

The Rod

The rod is seen as a neutral object, not to be identified with the person administering it. Parents should not use their hands, or those things that lead to personal identification. There should be no slapping or hitting with the hand. By following this practice, the child's fear will be directed toward the instrument of punishment and less toward the person. Otherwise, fear will be directed toward the person administering punishment.

My dad was a strong disciplinarian. He used various instruments of punishment, not always following the aforementioned rules. However, my dad's preferred instrument was a razor strap. He shaved with a straight razor, having this thick, two-ply, leather strap against which he stroked his razor in sharpening it. When he ministered punishment with that strap, let me tell you, I experienced pain. Consequently, when my dad approached me with the razor strap, I was transfixed, looking at the instrument and not my dad.

While rearing my children, I developed the habit of using a belt. When I trotted my boys off into private, as I doubled that belt, their eyes were not on me but on the belt.

Use a neutral instrument for corporal punishment in order that fear and bitterness will not be directed at the person, but rather toward the object used. Have you ever observed children who have been slapped by their parents? Mom or dad raises their hand, and they shrink in fear.

Instruction

The second facet of biblical discipline to be considered, first in priority but only second in our consideration, is found in the Hebrew word translated *instruction*, a word that at times means, and is translated *convince, convict*, to *prove*, or to *reprove*. Here is the next important and essential part of biblical discipline. If one administers nothing but the rod or lashing of the tongue, the result is harassment and not true biblical discipline.

One really begins to understand the true biblical approach to this subject through an understanding of Paul's instructions to the Ephesians found in chapter six of that letter. Suppose we consider the parts of Paul's words found in verse four.

Do Not

He begins with these words, *"And you fathers, do not provoke your children to wrath."*

When a dad administers the rod of chastisement in anger or wrath, that action results in rebellion, leading to resentment and reaction.

How does a father provoke his children to wrath? He does so by improperly administering chastisement in wrath, anger, impatience, abusiveness, and excessiveness, either in word or actions.

Do

We observe that Paul does not stop with the negative, but continues by telling fathers or parents what to do— *"but bring them up in the training (nurture) and admonition of the Lord."*

We understand the Apostle's thrust by subjecting two words to scrutiny and definition—training (nurture) and admonition.

The word translated *"training"* (nurture in the KJV) contains the meaning of chastisement. Vine, in his *Dictionary of New Testament Words,* writes that "nurture" denotes the *training* of a child, which includes *instruction,* further suggesting that Christian discipline regulates character. Training includes instruction and also involves chastisement.

Next, consider the Greek word translated *"admonition,"* the word *"nouthesna"* (verb "noutheo"), which means *putting in mind or training by word,* in this case the Word of God.

With these two words in mind, Paul is telling us, Fathers, don't provoke your children to wrath by just administering the rod to them, but in proper chastisement, take the Word of God and place it in their minds. One cannot have true Scriptural discipline that is not balanced by both chastisement and instruction.

Summary

In summarizing what has just been considered, we look to Proverbs, "My son, do not despise the chastening of the Lord, nor detest His correction; *For whom the Lord loves*

He corrects, Just as a father the son in whom he delights"
(Proverbs 3:11-12, emphasis added).

The Hebrew language in this text emphasizes that discipline is to be based on instruction, thus providing a vital Christian principle.

First of all, there must be instruction, the establishment of standards and principles by which one can determine what is right and what is wrong. These standards and principles become the basis upon which the rod is administered. There is a reversal, a distortion of biblical punishment or discipline, if we place the rod before instruction.

We do not chastise on the basis of mood or whim. So often when parents are irritated, when their children have offended them in some way, not necessarily having done something wrong, they chastise them. Parents are not to act in this fashion. It is only when there has been a transgression of the standards and principles established by instruction, then and only then, are parents to administer the rod.

Second, just as the Lord corrects those whom He loves, so also parents. What potent words are these, *"For whom the Lord loves He corrects; Just as a father the son in whom he delights."* If parents love their children, if they delight in them, they will exercise well-balanced discipline!

We read in Proverbs, chapter 29, verse 15, *"the rod and rebuke give wisdom."* There they are, both rod and rebuke or reproof. Both are essential. Without them we are told in that same context, *"But a child left to himself brings shame to his mother."* Where this balance is present, child abuse will not be an issue.

Thus, it is discovered why it is so important that children be subjected to discipline, for the lack of it will lead ultimately to the destruction of the family unit and will ultimately lead to bitter fruit in the life of the individual child.

Notes

1. *San Jose Mercury News*, 5 March 1979.

2. John Dewey, *Democracy and Education*, 1916.

3. Benjamin Spock, *Dr. Spock's Baby and Child Care*, Pocket Books, 1946.

4. *Seattle Times*, 17 March 1998.

5. *Wall Street Journal*, 22 September 1999.

Chapter Eleven

The Rod of Love
Part Two

In the face of children's violence, the lack of meaning of life for them and the excessive permissiveness of parents, let us continue our consideration of the role that "the rod of love" can play in helping solve these problems.

We found in the Columbine tragedy that the parents of the perpetrators of violence did not even know what their children were doing as they made bombs and prepared their firearms.

Parents, in their permissiveness, being consumed with the pleasures of this world, often demonstrate a lack of concern about what is transpiring in the lives of their children. Children involved in what has been called "the blackboard jungle," smoke marijuana, shoot dope, indulge in sexual liaisons, and much more without parents being concerned enough to investigate the type of lifestyle their children are living.

Many school administrators and teachers turn a blind eye or even worse contribute to the excesses of their students. Propounding relativistic values, they condone perverted lifestyles, sanction teenage sex, and teach them how to avoid adverse consequences rather than values, which would eliminate those excesses.

Now, what has just been written is a generalization and does not apply to all children, parents, school administrators, and teachers, probably to only a minority. However, the problems of the minority infect the bloodstream of life of the majority, with many falling prey to abuses and violence.

Thus we continue our consideration of the biblical concept of discipline, and how it is applied in the rod of love; determining yet another part of the solution to the problem.

The Procedure

We began the exploration of the problem and God's plan for parental discipline of their children in the previous chapter. We want to continue looking at the procedure involved in administering the rod of love, applying a number of biblical principles.

Begin Early

Notice that the administration of the rod, meaning balanced biblical discipline, should begin early in life. Looking back at that great book of wisdom, we begin by focusing on Proverbs, chapter 13, verse 24, considered briefly in the preceding chapter. Remember that we were told,

"He who spares his rod hates his son, *But he who loves him disciplines him promptly [early]*" (emphasis added).

The word translated *"promptly"* comes from a word originally meaning *"going after something early,"* as indicated in the margin of the NKJV. As used in this particular context, it would indicate that discipline should be applied early in the life of the child, this truth being found in Proverbs, chapter 19, verse 18, where we read, *"Chasten your son while there is hope and do not set your heart on his destruction."*

"Chasten your son while there is hope," we are told. Help in understanding what our inspired writer meant will be found in part in the book of Deuteronomy. We find instructions telling parents that, if they have a stubborn and rebellious son who refuses to obey his father or the voice of his mother, even after he is chastened, they are to take him to the elders of the city, who will in turn, *"stone him to death with stones"* (Deuteronomy 21:18-21).

Rather harsh treatment, wouldn't you agree? Yet the picture discovered here is that of a child who has been chastised, corrected, and disciplined by his parents, but still refuses to respond. The implication is that this condition is persistent, the individual continuing later in rebellion. The portrait is of one who is incorrigible.

No matter how harsh one considers this to be, a vital principle emerges as this passage is considered in connection with Proverbs, chapter 19, verse 18. Discipline the child early, deal with the rebellious spirit early while he is malleable, and avoid the child's destruction. Deal with the problem early enough, and the problem of rebellion can be resolved.

The Old Testament solution to the long-range problem of rebellion was designed in order that multitudes of generations would not be destroyed. Rebellion would be cut off at its source. The passage is not dealing with simple disobedience, but with unabated, incorrigible, and continuing rebellion—an extreme case. The wisdom of such seemingly harsh action is given in the concluding words of verse twenty-one, *"So you shall put away evil from among you, and all Israel shall hear and fear,"* thus a long range solution.

Chastise *early* in life so as to avoid later problems, even the possibility of death. The question arises here—when is early? At what point in the child's life should discipline begin? If I suggest to you that parents should begin with the infant child, many would protest in the light of seeming harshness. Yet, parents failing to start early invite disaster.

Here is the time of the greatest learning periods in life. It is beyond our ability to determine the capacity for learning of the infant child, for a baby to learn. I was shocked years ago when I read about how they were teaching babies in their early months to swim. My immediate response was that such would be impossible, not understanding how a small baby could learn to swim. And yet, there was the account with pictures of babies paddling and swimming in the water!

The point being made is that early childhood, even infancy, is a fantastically valuable time for learning. Once again, let us be reminded that the subject is not abuse nor excess of any kind, but reasonable discipline that should involve a measure of pain. The Hebrew word with which we are dealing refers to discipline that involves pain. A reasonable parent should be able to make an acceptable application of this principle.

A consideration of this subject is vital, for rebellion in our society has become a way of life, a condition resulting from permissiveness and humanistic relativity. The permissiveness that we are considering begins in the home with parents, where parents fail to discipline their children, which concludes with failure to punish lawbreakers in our society.

Susanna Wesley forever stands as one of the most outstanding, if not the most outstanding, among mothers about whom we know anything. Susanna Wesley gave birth to nineteen children, among whom were John and Charles, the founders of Methodism. Our civilization would have been impoverished without their leadership and teaching as champions of the faith. James Hefley said in relation to Susanna Wesley, *"Discipline was the word that most characterized her home-school. John began reading Genesis at the age of five, progressing rapidly to Greek, Latin, Hebrew, mathematics, and history."*

John's and Charles' mother disciplined her children *early* in life. She said, *"the self-willed child must be broken and subjected before he reaches the age of two years. He must know by then that his will must yield to his parents word and authority."*

One would suspect that a vast majority of parents would believe that discipline should really begin after age two, believing otherwise the child is too young. Yet, here is a great mother who achieved such great success that she can tell us, out of experience, that discipline must be applied and submission must already be taught to the children, including the "rod of love," before they reach the age of two!

One of her famed twenty-one principles for rearing children— *"When turned to a year old, some before then they were taught to fear the rod and cry softly. By which means they escaped an abundance of correction which they might otherwise have had."* Susanna Wesley was emphasizing that, by an administration of "the rod of love" before the age of one, many problems were avoided in the lives of her children.

One can just hear a great cry of protest going up, declaring Susanna Wesley's cruelty, abuse, and error. Today she would be thrown in the clinker, with the key thrown away. The "professionals" of our day would declare her mad. Yet, before one can do so, they must provide such living trophies as John and Charles Wesley, who shook the world for Christ, an influence that continues to this day and beyond!

The Bible says, *"Discipline your child [early] while there is hope."*

Consistency

Proper and successful discipline must be *consistent*. What is wrong yesterday is wrong today. Action that warranted administration of the rod yesterday still warrants the same today. Parents, to be successful, must teach principles and establish standards upon which the future of the child's life can be built.

For example, my dad had a rule that whenever my brother or I played with matches, with fire, a "whipping" was automatic. I inherited that principle and applied it to my own children. The principle was clearly stated to them, and throughout the rearing of my children was always applied, "when you play with matches or fire," I told my children, "a whipping is automatic. There is no court of appeal. There is no debate or excuse."

One Sunday when I returned home from church, there were five boys in the garage playing with matches. I don't even recall who they were! There was a foster son, his brother, a nephew, and my oldest son, at least these as I recall. I restated the rule, lined them up, and gave them a licking! Do you think they resented that action? Did it warp their psyche? They chuckle about the lesson learned to this very day.

We must be consistent in our application of the "rod of love." In addition, we are to be firm in our action, yet gentle and loving as we give reproof, correction, and instruction—giving a loving, careful explanation about why the rod is applied—all of this in order that future, serious problems may be avoided.

Yet, we teach inconsistency today on a nationwide basis, teaching by example that standards and punishment are all relative, with variable consequences, even when punishment takes place. We see hardened criminals, rapists, and sexual molesters committing heinous crimes, being permitted to go free because of some minute technicality. Even if they stand convicted, they are often back on the street after a brief time, committing the same crimes again. A convicted criminal can be sentenced to "life" in prison and be free in as little as seven years. Others who have been sentenced to death, remain on death row fourteen, fifteen years, delaying execution of their sentence.

The laxity and inconsistency in levying and carrying out punishment, in the legal and judicial realm, sets a bad example for the youth, encouraging them to test authority, feeling that such inconsistency will work in their favor.

The "rod of love," if it is to be successful in curbing youthful excess, must be administered in a consistent manner.

Firm

The application of discipline must also be *firm*. In other words, apply the rod firmly, in such a way that pain results. If parents threaten their children with the rod, a little tap or smack that doesn't exact pain will only encourage further disobedience.

The moment parents fail in being firm, and failing to carry out their threat with firmness, their children are taught to scorn discipline, annulling respect for the word of their parents. Again, as we saw earlier, here is precisely our attitude toward criminal law. A life sentence means all of life to me, but when it is made to mean seven years, imagine what kind of message such an application of law sends. Criminals hold our laws in scorn, ridicule, and contempt. Statistics were released some time ago, which indicated that "four out of five crimes are committed by ex-convicts!"

Keep in mind that the Bible teaches that we are driving out foolishness when the rod is applied. If that goal is to be accomplished, application will require firmness. Yet, on the other hand, it is to be gentle also, including instruction with tongue or in reproof.

Proverbs, chapter 15, verse 4 and 5, enunciate just such a principle. We find in verse five that the tongue is to be *"wholesome"* or *"healing."* Such a use of the tongue will enable parents to apply reproof or instruction gently. Thus a *"wholesome tongue is a tree of life"* — a wholesome, gentle, healing tongue.

Otherwise, *"perverseness in it [the tongue] breaks the spirit"* (verse 4b). Perverse means harsh or bitter use of the tongue. We find that a profane, a harsh, and perverse tongue crushes and breaks the spirit. Parents are not to lash their children in reproof and instruction with harsh speech, bitter and profane words.

Parents are never to demean their children, calling them "stupid," saying "you are dumb," or any words or names that are demeaning, degrading, and imply dislike of the individual. Actions may be condemned, but not the "actor."

So, apply the rod firmly, but gently.

Enforce Rules

Discipline should be carried out when threatened. However, on the other side of the coin, do not make a threat unless you intend to keep your word. If parents threaten chastisement and fail to keep their word, children will not respect the word of their parents. One often hears parents saying, "I've told you before and I'm not going to tell you again," repeating the same line over and over. Disobedience then results and they wonder why. On the other hand, if the parents finally fulfill their threat and punish the child, the child feels that the punishment is unfair since he has gotten away with that very thing so many times previously.

Apply the Rod in Private

Carry out punishment in private. Love will seek to avoid humiliating the child. Whenever I disciplined my children, even in strong verbal reproof, I did not subject them to embarrassment in the presence of others. When the rod was administered in corporal punishment, I always did so in privacy. I never wanted them to even be in the company of other family members, much less the company of their friends and others, avoiding humiliating them. Parents are to secure submission and not humiliation.

Submission

When children are brought into submission to the will of parents, they should not be permitted to cry in anger. If a child is permitted to cry in anger during punishment, the cry is an expression of rebellion, and submission has not been accomplished.

Remember the words of Susanna Wesley? She taught her children to fear the rod, and cry softly, not in anger.

Affection

Parents should *always* show affection and *never* discipline in anger. Children should know that what is being done is done in love, not just because the parent is irritated or offended.

A suggestion to parents—if you will administer discipline to your children, observing the previous principle, you will observe a profound influence in their lives. Why? Because the plan is God's, founded on His Word.

A Lack of Discipline

When there is a lack of discipline, the results will be disobedience and lawlessness. An examination of the example of the Prophet Eli and his two sons, as found in 1 Samuel, chapter 2, will clearly validate and substantiate that statement.

As we examine Eli's relationship with his sons Hophnes and Phinehas, we will discover examples of what happens when biblical discipline is not exercised.

Results of Disobedience

When standards of right and wrong are not known or enforced through instruction, when the admonition of the Lord is not given as indicated in Ephesians, chapter 6, verse 4, disobedience results. When the words of God are not placed into the minds of children, rebellion is sure.

With these thoughts in mind, consider the words of 1 Samuel, chapter 2, verse 12, where we read, *"Now the sons of Eli were corrupt (literally: sons of Belial); they did not know the Lord."* As "Sons of Belial," they were corrupt and worthless. Why? Because as we have just read, "they did not know the Lord."

Here we see the consequences resulting from parent's indifference or failure in bringing their children up to "know the Lord."

Many parents have said to me, "I will not make my children go to church." These and others have added, "I will not force anything on my children, but I will permit them to grow up and make up their own minds."

What happens when parents have such an attitude and fail to teach and direct their children? If that practice is followed, by the time they grow up without firm direction, their rebellion will be firmly set.

I had the privilege of directing my 60-year-old brother-in-law to Christ, for whom my wife Jean had been praying and to whom she had been witnessing for thirty years. He had resisted her witness steadfastly, in numerous misconceptions, views that were firmly set.

Why did Ken hold these views until the age of sixty? He did so because he was not given the truth when he was a child, young, responsive and pliable. If parents do not teach their children truth about God, and fail to restrain them from rebellion, the result will be a generation of Hophnes and Phinehas—exactly what we are observing today.

Parent's first responsibility is to introduce their children to Christ, set standards of conduct, and teach them God's ways.

Lawlessness

When children are permitted to indulge in fleshly desires unrestrained, when foolishness is not driven out with "the rod of love," a spirit of disobedience and *lawlessness* results. Consider the example of Hophne and Phinehas as found in 1 Samuel, chapter 2, verses 13 through 17.

Their father Eli had failed to restrain them. Consequently, when they were given the privilege of obtaining food just like the priests, their lawless attitude was revealed. The priest's servant would dip flesh hooks into the boiling meat that had been sacrificed, and whatever clung to the flesh hooks belonged to the priest for food. However, that wasn't good enough for Hophne and Phinehas, as they demanded raw meat to be roasted.

When food was offered to these two "sons of Belial" in the prescribed way, their response was, *"Give meat for roasting to the priest, for he will not take boiled meat from you, but raw."* If their will was resisted, the two would answer, *"No, but you must give it now [the raw meat for roasting]; and if not, I will take it by force!"* Thus we are told that *"the sin of the young men was very great before the Lord, for men abhorred the offering of the Lord."*

The root of the whole problem is discovered in the words found in 1 Samuel, chapter 3, verse 13, *"his sons made themselves vile and **he did not restrain them.**"* (emphasis added) Eli had not restrained them from exercising their bents toward evil.

Evil Results

When parents fail to control their children, when they fail to bring them into submission, evil results.

The prophet Eli did not even know what his sons were doing, having to find out from others. He said to Hophne and Phinehas, *"Why do you do such things? For I hear of your evil dealings from all the people"* (1 Samuel 2:23).

One will discover from Paul's letter to Timothy, 1 Timothy, chapter 3, verse 4, that the man of God is to *"manage his own household well."* That word *"manage"* means to *"stand before and lead,* keeping under control," a military term literally meaning to fall into rank under a higher authority. So parents are to be out front with an exemplary life in order to say to their children, "Fall in and follow me!"

A Lack of Respect

Not only do disobedience and lawlessness result when parents fail to give proper leadership to their children, but a lack of respect for authority results from such neglect.

Recall that the Bible teaches in Ephesians, chapter 6, verse 1, that children are to *"obey your parents in the Lord, for this is right."* However, the admonition does not end with obedience only, but continues with instructions to *"Honor your father and mother, which is the first commandment with promise."*

Obedience alone is not enough. Children are also to honor and respect their parent's authority. Hophne and Phinehas had not been taught, nor had they learned respect for authority.

There is such a lack of respect in this area today, from adults and children alike. Policemen are called "fuzz" and "pigs." That disrespect, on the part of children, has been learned from their parents. Thus, they reap a bitter harvest today as violence and "death goes to school," as children look with disdain, dishonor, and disrespect at figures of authority.

Adding insult to injury, so many leaders and people in authority, including parents, demonstrate such disrespect in their own lives and set such poor examples, the children have few role models to follow! Once again, the problem rests with parents and other leaders. Today's children are products of that leadership!

A Lack of Submission

Disobedience and lawlessness result when parents fail to develop a spirit of submission in their children. Looking to the example of Eli and his sons once again, we are reminded of these words as God said to Eli, *"For I have told him that I will judge his house forever for the iniquity which he knows, because his sons made themselves vile, and he did not restrain them"* (1 Samuel 3:13).

The Lord said to Eli, I will judge your house forever. Why? Because his sons were vile, and Eli *"restrained them not."* We tend to judge Hophne and Phinehas severely, but their problem began with the seeming indifference and neglect of their father Eli. He was so busy being a prophet that he ignored his responsibility to his sons, failing to teach them submission to the Lord, as well as to himself. Parents should learn a profound lesson here—one can be so wrapped up in doing "good" that he ignores his family duties!

Furthermore, a child who is reared in an undisciplined home will probably reproduce the same in his own home. Consider the example of the prophet Samuel as found in 1 Samuel, chapter 8. This great prophet, unquestionably a great man of God, had grown up under the supervision of Eli. As a result we read concerning Samuel's sons in verse three, *"But his sons did not walk in his ways; they turned aside after dishonest gain, took bribes and perverted justice."*

Summary

The Christian Alternative to humanistic "Children's Liberation" must include the biblical pattern for discipline, "the rod of love."

The biblical pattern will cause parents to—one, lead their children to Christ; two, tolerate no fleshly sin; three, exert proper leadership and keep the household under control; four, teach their children to respect authority; and five, develop a spirit of submission in their children.

If parents fail in these endeavors, permitting their children to "do their own thing," the result will be the destruction of the family and a generation of Hophnes and Phinehas'— exactly the results we now experience!

Is what has been said unloving? Certainly not, because God's pattern for the parent-child relationship is patterned after His relationship and discipline of His children. As the Bible says, *"Whom the Lord loves, He chastens."*

Chapter Twelve

Training For Life in Canaan

"We are a separate people with our own standards and they must never be fused into one. I cannot make you happy or unhappy, but I can make myself happy. I accept my ultimate aloneness and responsibility for myself."

No, these are not the words of the author, but as we saw earlier, words from a suggested marriage contract appearing in a women's magazine. These words are repeated here so as to demonstrate the self-centeredness and selfishness that is represented in secular humanism, as exemplified in the extreme movements of women's and children's liberation.

As has been discovered, those movements, with their self-centeredness, are designed for the destruction of the traditional two-parent family unit. The Christian alternative to such a philosophy is to recognize that the family is a unit, in which every family member has a specific role and responsibility to fulfill in their familial relationships.

Our emphasis in this context, in dealing with the parent-child relationship, has been to focus on the responsibility of parents for their children in every area of life.

We now arrive at the parent's responsibility for teaching and preparing the children to honor God and how to live

155

successfully in a wicked world. In making the determination regarding *how* this responsibility is to be carried out, the book of Deuteronomy, chapter 6 will provide the answer.

Get the setting clearly in mind regarding the prevailing circumstances at the time these words were written by Moses. The children of Israel are poised, ready to enter into Canaan, the Promised Land. In spite of the fact that this land is to contain tremendous blessings, yet Israel will be confronted by terrible problems.

The Canaanites are there, steeped in idolatry and having heinous sin, like the sin of Sodom and Gomorrah. The children of Israel could overcome them, but on the other hand they could be overcome by them, falling prey to the Canaanite lifestyle, thus becoming similarly decadent.

Consequently, God is giving instructions through His servant Moses on how to live in Canaan in a way which is pleasing to Him, while not falling prey to their lifestyle and decadence.

Parents today need the same kind of instruction, for their children are faced with the challenge of living successfully in a wicked world. How will they be able to survive and not fall prey to the humanistic excesses that surround them?

My wife and I, seeing the excesses, the decadence that exists, observing the decay, wondered how our children could survive as they were growing up, wondering what was in store for them. Now we are equally concerned for our grandchildren, as we observe decadence sweeping the world like a southwestern tornado, destroying everything in its path, leaving the ruins of immorality and death behind.

In the face of such a challenge, similar to that faced by Moses and the children of Israel, the need is to find the answer of how children will be able to survive and not be overwhelmed by this world system. In determining how such success is possible, we investigate the instructions of how under the topic, *"Training for Life in Canaan."*

Basic instructions are found in the first four verses of this great chapter:

Now this is the commandment, and these are the statutes and judgments which the Lord your God has commanded to teach you, that you may observe them in the land which you are crossing over to possess, that you may fear the Lord your God , to keep all His statutes and His commandments which I command you, you and your son and your grandson, all the days of your life and that your days may be prolonged.

Therefore hear, O Israel, and be careful to observe it, that it may be well with you and that you may multiply greatly as the Lord God of your fathers has promised you—a land flowing with milk and honey.

Hear, O Israel: The Lord our God, the Lord is one!

Moses is saying in effect, you will be strangers in Canaan, faced with the wickedness of the Canaanites, who have their false gods, Astarte, Baal, and Molech. The first thing to be remembered is that the Lord our God is the One and only God, and He alone must be worshipped, rejecting the false gods of the land. Keep the commandments, the statutes, and the judgment of the one true God in order that it may go well with you, and that you may increase mightily. If they did this, the indication was that the land would become a land of promise, flowing with milk and honey, just as God promised.

The Canaanites did not know God, Moses would say, and we can add, neither do the majority of the people of the world of our day. Therefore, the basic training that is needed,

157

in our relationship with God, if we are to know and do His will and fulfill his plan for our lives, comes in the following words found in verse five through seven.

The basic instruction in verse five is, *"You shall love the Lord your God with all your heart, with all your soul, and with all your strength."*

The Canaanites were dedicated to Israel's destruction just as the present world system is dedicated to ours. Moses was saying that Canaan will seek to liberate your children from the love of God, in order that they be enslaved to the debauchery of Astarte and Baal. Consequently, you must love God with your total ability.

So parents, here is the way you are to teach your children, teaching them a love of God that permeates all of life.

The Responsibility of Parents

As one examines verses six and seven, the truth emerges that teaching about God, truth, right and wrong, is the responsibility of parents. Listen parents, *"and these words which I command you this today shall be in your heart. **You** shall teach them diligently to your children."*

Words Alone Are Not Enough

Parents will never be able to communicate what they do not have themselves. *"These words shall be in your heart."* Parents must have the truth, model it in their lives, before they can effectively teach their children. Whatever is taught will be filtered through the grid of the teacher's life. Parents can never hope to communicate anything to their children that they do not possess themselves. Inconsistency in the parent's life will cancel out the validity of anything they may say.

The truth being expressed here is like the old saying attributed to Thoreau, that what you are doing speaks so loudly that I cannot hear what you are saying.

The only valid approach is found in Paul's letter to the Philippians, chapter 4, verse 9, *"The things which you have learned and received and heard and seen in me, these do, and the God of peace will be with you."* Paul emphasized that, it is not only what you have heard, but what you have seen me do. Parents, and we emphasize again, will never be able to teach their children successfully unless they can say to them first of all, "those things which you have seen in me, do!" Do as I do.

Furthermore, consider his words to the Corinthian Christians as found in 1 Corinthians, chapter 7, verse 1, *"Imitate me, just as I also imitate Christ."* Paul instructs them literally to imitate, to mimic his lifestyle, just as he imitated the life of Christ.

Rules and Regulations Not Enough

Lists of rules and regulations in this life will not be enough unless one can say, what you have seen modeled in my life, what has been evident in my life, do!

Parents first teach by what is in their lives, both in word and deed. For example, children are not sent to Sunday school with the intention of passing the teaching responsibility to the Sunday school teacher. Parents begin by bringing them to Sunday school, placing a premium upon learning themselves.

Consequently, number one, parents cannot teach something they don't have themselves; number two, teaching is the parent's responsibility, as observed in Deuteronomy, chapter 6, verse 7 — *"And you shall teach them diligently to your children."*

Teaching is not the state's responsibility, the school's responsibility, or even the pastor's responsibility. Teaching is the duty of parents! Thus, whatever other teaching takes place is delegated by the parents, and where the parents convictions are transgressed by those to whom teaching is delegated, the parents should promptly take action to remove their children from that influence.

Yet we find that the state is endeavoring to usurp this responsibility, pretending that they alone can solve the problems afflicting our children, schools, and society. "Education" is the key word of the politician, who is also referring to the state's assuming total control in this area. Valueless education is presented as a panacea of all of our problems, with the state assuming educational responsibility through day care, head start, and the total learning span of a child's life.

> *Ever since its inception in 1965, Head Start, the government subsidized preschool program, has been touted by two generations of politicians as a cure to a wide variety of social ills: delinquency, teen pregnancy, unemployment, drug use and welfare dependency. Put a child on the right track, so the thinking goes, and the rest will largely take care of itself. Now Vice President Gore, wishing to extend the program's reach, has made universal preschool education one of the centerpieces of his family-oriented campaign agenda. But before he or anyone else starts writing legislation, we need to consider why we are offering preschool in every pot, and exactly what it is that we are offering.*[1]

Just sample the prevailing state philosophy through such words as these spoken by Dr. Mary Jo Bane, Associate Director of Wellesley College Center for Research on Women. Bane said, *"We really don't know how to raise children. The fact that children are raised in families means that* *there is no equality. **In order to raise children with equality, we must take them away from families and raise them.*** (emphasis added)

What unmitigated drivel from this women's lib advocate. I don't know what kind of doctor she is, but she doesn't use very good grammar. We don't *"raise"* children. We may raise chickens or corn or cotton, but we *rear* children. However, Mary Jo really chooses her words well, indicating just what the goal of the women's lib and humanistic state is—a determination to destroy the traditional family unit, seeing children as *"things,"* to *raise,* supplanting traditional family values with those of human relativism.

Way back on 22 December 1978, the Associated Press reported how James Roy, a Baptist minister, forbade his daughter, because of Christian convictions, not to attend dances or wear slacks. His daughter disobeyed, whereupon Roy spanked her with a shingle, a very thin piece of wood. As a result, as reported by the Associated Press, the Onondaga County Family Court in New York took the daughter away from her father, stipulating that she would only be permitted to return to the family if the daughter was permitted to do whatever she wanted to do, without fear of punishment, as though the absence of slacks or dances might destroy the poor girl's life!

In spite of all that is transpiring, God charges parents with the responsibility of teaching their children. Parents need to have this truth drilled into their minds, that is, that they are to *"diligently"* teach their children! An understanding of what such teaching involves comes in an understanding of precisely what the Hebrew word translated *"diligently"* means. The word used means *"to whet"* or *"to sharpen,"* thus, the admonition is to sharpen your children, make them sharp and discerning.

Moses is not talking just about imparting fact, but he is talking about *the truth* which is "caught as well as taught."

He is not talking about just dispensing information, which may be dry as powder, revolting to the taste, but is talking about the way to live a life so sharp that the child is able to discern error from truth.

The words of Hebrews, chapter 4, verse 12, will be readily remembered here— *"For the word of God is living and powerful, and sharper than any two-edged sword, piercing even to the division of soul and spirit, and of joints and marrow, and is a discerner of the thoughts and intents of the heart."*

We recognize that the Word of God, the "Sword of the Spirit," is living, sharp, and powerful, able to make the children sharp. Parents need to give their children the "living word," not just cold, dull rules that dull their spiritual sensitivity, dry facts that lodge in their spiritual throats. When parents fulfill this command, their children will be turned on rather than turned off.

Kip Kinkel, 17-year-old former Thurston High School student, who in May, 1999, turned his gun on a roomful of his Springfield, Oregon high school classmates, killing two and wounding twenty-six, changed his plea of insanity to guilty. Kinkel told a psychiatrist that he believed he was an embarrassment to his parents because he wasn't perfect. Kinkel reportedly told psychiatrist Dr. Orin Balstad, *"I had to be 100 percent perfect. No one is perfect though. Lots of times, life sucked. With my parents, if I didn't do my best, I was an embarrassment to my parents."*[2]

Kinkel shot and killed his father, after being suspended from school, and after telling his mother, "I love you, Mom," he shot and killed her.

What is known from these facts seems to indicate that Kip's parents fell into the trap of giving "cold rules," perhaps administering the rod without love, gentleness, and understanding. One could conclude that here were teaching methods gone wrong, methods that violate the principles just enumerated. Rules and regulations alone are not enough!

Yet, parents encounter tremendous problems in knowing how to teach their children, there being so much contradictory information available about how to deal with, how to train, how to discipline children, from Dewey to Spock, even Ann Landers!

Ann Landers, you ask. Yep, Ann Landers has pitched in permitting her views in this area to be known. My son Stephen, while still in school, asked one day, "Dad, did you read Ann Landers?" Since I've never made it a practice to read her columns, I had to answer "no." Well, Stephen said, "Ann Landers says it doesn't do any good to spank your children." I replied, "On the basis of experience, what do you think?" With a little grin, Stephen answered that "it did some good!" I suggested that he write Ann Landers and straighten her out!

The point is—there is a great diversity of information about how to rear and deal with children in discipline. In spite of the effort of one writer, to whom I referred earlier, one who wrote discounting the Bible because it was "a book written at the time of the pharaohs," I still turn to the Bible. The gentlemen's comments actually validate that the teaching of the Bible has stood the test of time.

Consequently, we hearken back to Proverbs, chapter 22, verse 6, and sample the wisdom found there regarding training children. *"Train up a child,"* the inspired writer begins. Remember how that terminology referred to the inside of the mouth, terminology used in describing the practice of the midwife. The midwife would take a sweet substance and massage the gums and mouth of the newly born baby, creating a taste and hunger so that the baby would begin sucking, ready to be fed by mother's milk.

What wonderful imagery! Parents are to teach in this fashion, sharpening their children, whetting their appetites, and creating in them a taste for and a delight in the things of God.

The Teaching Process

Consider the *teaching process* as outlined in Moses' instruction found in Deuteronomy, chapter 6. The process is clearly delineated, beginning with verse seven and continuing through nine, you sit in your house, when you walk by the way, when you lie down, and when you rise up.

You shall teach them diligently to your children, and shall talk of them when

You shall bind them as a sign on your hand, and they shall be as frontlets between your eyes. You shall write them on the doorposts of your house and on your gates.

Teach

Parents begin by teaching their children about the commandments, statutes, and judgments of God. That teaching is to be diligent, a regular ministering of the Word of God.

Just how that teaching continues in a diligent fashion is essential to know, if parents are to succeed. "You shall *teach* them diligently to your children, and shall *talk* of them." Parents are to talk to their children about God and good. When does this talk take place? It happens when you sit in your house, when you walk by the way, when you lie down, and when you get up in the morning.

These words reveal when and where the teaching process is to take place. Parents are not told to preach to their children, lecture their children, but simply talk to them, the most simple and normal way of teaching, really the pattern exemplified by Jesus as He taught His disciples (though there were recorded times of structured settings for formal instruction, such as the Sermon on the Mount).

After all, here is what we do if we want to meaning-fully communicate with a loved one or friend. One does not sit down and preach to a friend, lecture a friend, but simply converses with him.

Perhaps here is the greatest failure of parents. They fail to spend time just talking with their children about the most important issues of life. Parents talk about nonessentials but are inclined to lecture when it comes to essentials—brief lectures at that. Perhaps the greatest failure relates to spiritual issues. Do parents really feel comfortable in talking *with* their children about spiritual matters? We are inclined to departmentalize our lives. When it comes to spiritual matters, we set those apart like, "now hear this, I have a spiritual pronouncement I want to make." Once the pronouncement is made, we move on to the secular, which normally dominates our lives.

Moses said, don't do that! The Canaanites have removed God from their lives. You are not to do that. Talk about God and His way in such a fashion that it permeates all of your life. In other words, Moses is emphasizing that God and His commandments are not to be excluded from any area or time frame of life.

But what have we done in reality? "Religious" people can't talk about government, governmental leaders, or legislation because that is "politics," and we are told not to talk about that, because "politics" and "religion" don't mix. One person struck at the heart of such error, saying, "If your politics don't mix with religion, there's something terribly wrong with your politics."

A big sign has been placed over certain areas of life, including the political realm and government, that says, "God, keep out. This area is off limits. Stay out of the classroom." An excellent example of how efforts have been made to exclude God from public life may be seen in this effort made by The American Civil Liberties Union (ACLU).

Since the terrorist attacks on the World Trade Center on September 11, 2001, the song *God Bless America* has bee heard regularly in public events: in the halls of government, before and during ball games, on radio and television, in churches – North, East, South, and West..

However, the ACLU has protested and challenged the words, *God Bless America* when they have appeared in school, demanding that they be removed, with success in some cases. One school reportedly removed the words, with another even ceasing to repeat the Pledge of Allegiance because it contains the words *one nation under God.*

The Breen Elementary School in Rocklin, California, a small city near the State Capitol, Sacramento, placed the words *God Bless America* on its sign marquee in front of the school. The ACLU protested and demanded that the words be removed, reported the *Auburn Journal* (October 11, 2001). The *San Francisco Chronicle* (October 13, 2001) reported that Margaret Crosby of the Northern Chapter of the ACLU called the sign "hurtful" and "divisive," alleging that it was a violation of the U.S. Constitution and was dividing its young students along religious lines. Crosby said the sign "must be replaced immediately."

To the School's credit, the School Board and Administration rejected the protest, calling the assertion made by the ACLU "absurd."

Nevertheless, through such perverted interpretation of the First Amendment, the ACLU and others have generally succeeded in removing God and any reference to God from the schools and the halls of government.

Consequently, Moses' admonition to parents to include God in all of their conversation, permit Him to permeate every area of life, has never been more relevant and essential than today.

Moses said, include God in all of your conversation, permit Him to permeate every area of life. When and where is this manner of communication to take place?

When You Sit in Your House

"You shall talk of them [God's words through Moses] as you sit in your house," words which reveal the first location of the children's learning center. But how many parents spend time just sitting in their houses, talking to their children? People live busy lives and are seldom home. As I make pastoral visits, I am often fortunate to find one out of five or six at home.

My life has been no exception, for I have, in the past, been seldom at home. I recall one night when I came home late, when my children were small, my wife said humorously, "Children, permit be to introduce you to your father." I justified my absence by being involved in serving the Lord, such a situation being no excuse in the majority of homes.

Yet, when the family members are all at home, what do they do? Perhaps they gather around the television set as it spews forth garbage, ungodly in nature, not fit for human consumption. If the electricity were to go off, or if something happened to the tube, we wonder what the family would do.

However, all of that aside, when parents and family members are home, when can the instructions given by Moses be best carried out? Actually, the choicest time for fellowship and meaningful communication is at mealtime, as the family gathers around the table to eat. Here is an informal time when talk flows freely, family members draw close and share their thoughts, often lingering long after the meal is finished.

When we desire to communicate with someone else in a meaningful fashion, what do we do? We make arrangements to share a meal with them. I wanted to have time with my pastor-son Chris just this past week, discussing some aspects of the ministry. To accommodate a meaningful time together, we chose to have lunch. (I paid the bill, of course!). I arrange to have lunch regularly with staff members, periods of time when we can communicate meaningfully. I set aside a time every week to take my wife out to eat, endeavoring to avoid any interference with those valuable times spent with her.

Eating together constitutes such a precious time in relation to fellowship, and a time for interaction of thoughts. Consider the example of the Master as He invites us, in these words found in Revelation, chapter 3, verse 20,

*"Behold, I stand at the door and knock. If anyone hears my voice and opens the door, I will come in to him **and dine with him**, and he with me."*

Our Savior Himself is using eating together to illustrate the choice fellowship and relationship available to *"anyone"* who will extend an invitation to Him.

Food and talk go together. Parents should not miss this opportunity. I confess that I failed miserably in this exercise and lost much because of it. Only my dear Father, with the faithfulness of my wife Jean, salvaged my children and gave wonderful victory in their lives as they live to serve Him today.

Parents should not get caught up in what we might call the gasoline filling-station syndrome, making the table only a place to come and fill-up!

When You Walk by the Way

Furthermore, Moses added, this verbal exchange is to continue as *"you walk by the way."* Parents need to walk and talk with their children, carrying on totally informal conversations, just enjoying one another's company. Moses is emphasizing that parents should simply talk about God and His word in a normal, informal way as they go from place to place.

But what is happening instead? Junior rushes off to little league, while Suzie rushes off to girl's softball, and mom hurries to Jazzercise. In efforts to keep occupied, family time has been so structured that there is little time left to talk. Dad says to son, how has your day been, Junior? Junior replies, I'm sorry dad, but I'm late for ball practice. Family members end up gulping down food so they can all go their separate ways.

Moses says, you just need to talk together about the Lord and His Word. Children need it, and suffer when that need is not fulfilled. One of my fine grandsons, away in Slovakia on a mission trip, was calling home with his sister. Kraegen said to his mother Shirley on the phone, "You know what I miss most of all? I miss our talks together!"

A majority of parents should admit that they know little about the things that trouble and concern their children, knowledge that would normally come in a natural way as they just talk together, in a way conducive to sharing, assuring them in actions and attitude that they are being heard sympathetically. How many parents really listen to their children? Children talk, but dad or mom don't hear a word they say. They say, "uhuh, yes, okay, good." When it's over, they haven't heard a word, and the children know it.

Parents would be amazed at what their children would share if only they would listen in concern. Moses said talk as you walk. These are teachable moments when sharing flows naturally in normal meaningful conversation about eternal things and values.

When You Lie Down

Parents, do your children come and crawl into bed with you just to talk? Oh, you may answer, they once did, but not anymore. At what age are they supposed to quit doing that? I don't know, but there were times when I came home late from work. My wife had gone to bed early just to read, and I would see my big old kids lying on the bed talking to their mother.

On the other hand, when children are younger, parents should make it a practice to lie down with them in bed. Just lie there in the dark and listen to them. You know, life has a way of getting down to its simplest common denominator as you lie there looking up in the darkness talking together. Parents might be surprised at the concerns of the day and the questions that will emerge there in the darkness, giving such wonderful opportunity for understanding, parental response that instructs so naturally and openly.

However, when you lie down with your children, you don't say, "Okay Junior, let's talk." No, you lovingly lie down with them. You might not say a word for a little while. You might say, "How has your day been? You know, I just wanted to let you know that I love you!"

In a situation or setting like that, a conversation will flow normally. Such a practice will solve and heal the troubled hearts of your children. One person said we should never permit our children to go to bed troubled, for when we do, those troubles are imprinted indelibly on their lives.

Moses said, talk with your children when they lie down and include conversation about spiritual values and matters. Such a practice was the norm when Moses penned these words, for families slept together in close quarters. Parents today must put forth extra effort in making this happen.

When You Rise Up

Finally Moses said, talk to your children *"when you rise up,"* the first thing in the morning when you get out of bed and start your day. I think Moses' emphasis is, talk to your children whenever the opportunity arises throughout the entire day; from the most pleasant to the most difficult times, just let the love of God permeate your lives and conversation.

Yet, another application we can draw from this text is, don't segregate your day into spiritual and secular sections. That danger leads to the idea that we put aside a time, say five minutes is God's and the other twenty-three hours and fifty-five minutes belong to us. Moses is saying that the entire twenty-four hours belong to God. He is included in our conversation when we get up, when we go about during the day, when we sit in the house, and when we lie down at night, all opportune times to sharpen the lives of our children within the normal context of living.

In a news article expressing concern about the influence of child care centers, Dr. Phyllis Levenstein, a professor at State University of New York at Stoneybrook, and director of the Verbal Interaction Project, is quoted as saying, *"The degree to which mothers converse with their children has an influence on IQ, reading, arithmetic, and creativity."* Dr. Levenstein further concluded, *"Where there is no human attachment there can be no conscience,"* and she added, *"that adults denied bonding form a large part of the criminal population."*[3]

One thing for sure that we discover in the Deuteronomy text is that the parents failure to talk to their children will have serious consequences in the area of spirituality, leaving the children unprepared for life in Canaan.

Summary

Look back to Deuteronomy, chapter 6, verses 8 and 9 for some concluding thoughts on this subject, *"You shall bind them [God's commandments and Word] upon your hand, and they shall be as frontlets between your eyes. You shall write them on the door posts of your house and your gates."*

Binding God's Word on your hand suggests that the principles involved will impact one's work life for good. Making the teaching of the law of God frontlets between the eyes, figurative language, indicates the impact such teaching will make on one's thought life. Writing them on the door posts of the house and on the gates emphasizes the influence that the truth will exert on the life, as the child departs from the home. The life and mind of the child will be sharpened, preparing for life in the world of Canaan.

When parents teach their children in such a fashion, their children will not only not forget God, but they will fear and revere Him, and come to serve Him.

The problem that afflicts us today is that life has been secularized, and God has been forgotten. When parents do this, secularize and separate their lives, excluding God from great segments of time by their actions and failures, they are declaring to their children that God is not really important.

The Christian alternative is to teach, to sharpen the lives of our children in order that their appetites will be for God and His Word.

Parents should consider these three questions:

One, do you love God and His Word, keeping His Word in your heart? If not, when you endeavor to teach your children what is not in your life, they will rebel.

Two, are you taking advantage of the normal opportunities of the day in teaching and sharpening the lives of your children, or have you segregated God out of great segments of your time?

Three, are you training by the way you live, as well as by the way you speak?

The Apostle Paul wrote to Timothy, 2 Timothy, chapter 3, verse 13, *"But evil men and impostors will grow worse and worse, deceiving and being deceived."* We live in a day like this described by Paul, in which "impostors" and "evil men" are growing worse, and deception is at work at every hand.

But the Apostle gives young Timothy the solution as we read,

"But you must continue in the things which you have learned and been assured of, knowing from whom you have learned them, and that from childhood you have known the Holy Scriptures, which are able to make you wise for salvation through faith which is in Christ Jesus" (2 Tim. 3:14-16).

Timothy, your life has been sharpened by your mother Eunice and your grandmother Lois (2 Tim. 1:5). You need not be deceived but be discerning, continuing in the things that you learned from your mother and grandmother, having come to know the Holy Scriptures from childhood, knowledge that has made you wise unto salvation. Here is the essence of what Paul said to Timothy.

Can we say that to our children? Can we say to them, from childhood you have known the Holy Scriptures? Only when parents can answer these questions in the affirmative, will their children be prepared for life in Canaan, in this evil world system of relativism and secular humanism.

Notes

1. *Wall Street Journal*, 8 July 1999.

2. *Los Angeles Times*, 25 September 1999.

3. *Santa Cruz Sentinel*, 17 June 1979.

Chapter Thirteen

Liberating Children
the Biblical Way

In Boulder, Colorado, 24-year-old Tom Hanson was suing his parents for $250,000, claiming it was his parent's fault that he had mental problems. Of course, it is the humanist view of children's liberation that leads to such action as this. Children suing their parents, even bringing charges for abuse in response to even gentle acts of discipline or spanking.

Our attention is drawn to the view of a humanist, "kiddie-libber," psychologist Richard Farson, who wrote in his article, *"Birthrights," "Children must have the guarantee of a fair trial with due process of law, an advocate to protect their rights against parents."* [1] It's interesting that children need legal protection against their parents, possibly so in rare cases, but not all children as Farson would advocate. Farson advocated that the *"liberated child of the future would include freedom from physical punishment, freedom to vote, total sexual freedom, economic freedom, and others!"*

The secularists', humanists', relativists' view of what constitutes "children's liberation" becomes quite clear in the words of Farson. Age becomes irrelevant. The liberated child is to be free of parental control, including economic freedom. Failure in providing such freedoms can subject the parent to legal action—prosecution for supposed parental failure or a civil suit for damages.

No wonder there are more and more acts of disobedience in school and society, some children running rampant in acts of violence in schools and gangs. Chaos, violence, and anarchy are normal outgrowths when children are given freedom before being prepared to act responsibly.

Consequently, it is imperative that we discover how parents can prepare their children for independence or freedom. Lack of such preparations inevitably lead to dire consequences.

Thus, our purpose is to determine how parents can properly liberate their children, considering the topic, "Liberating Children the Biblical Way."

The time will come when the child leaves home, making his or her own way in life. God has designed it to be so. The Bible says, *"Therefore a man shall leave his father and mother and be joined to his wife, and they shall become one flesh"* (Gen. 2:24).

The "leaving" may, and more often than not precedes the "cleaving." No matter the order involved, children must be prepared to "leave," for liberation, and that preparation should begin at birth.

Discovering God's Bent

The first step in preparing children for liberation is to *discover God's bent,* God's design for their lives.

Recall how parents are admonished to *"train up a child in the way he should go"* in Proverbs, chapter 22, verse 6. Another way of expressing this truth, consistent with the meaning and more understandable, is to say, *"train up a child in accordance with God's design for his or her life."*

Step One

In determining how to discover God's design for children, we would do well to observe the example set by Joseph and Mary in the life of Jesus.

We are told how, after Jesus' birth, before returning to Nazareth from Egypt, that Joseph and Mary, *"had performed all things according to the law of the Lord"* (Luke 2:39). Mary and Joseph began by fulfilling all of the things concerning the law and the plan of God in the child's life, rather than seeking to fulfill their own desires.

This truth brings to mind one reason why so many parents fall short in preparing their children for freedom and responsibility. They endeavor to fulfill their own aspirations in and through their children, many times endeavoring to compensate for their own failures, trying to make their children what they had desired to be, or actually are. In such a situation the child becomes an extension of the parent, making it difficult to set them free to be his or her own person.

Step Two

The next step in preparations for liberating the child, the biblical way, is to permit the child to develop naturally, with parents not pushing them into being what they think they ought to be or rushing them through life. The child should be permitted to develop naturally, according to God's plan.

Notice again the example of Jesus as found in Luke, chapter 2, and verse 40 where we are told *"the child grew and became strong in spirit, filled with wisdom."* As we see the words, *"the child grew,"* the indication is that Mary and Joseph permitted the child Jesus to develop naturally. Since He was a gifted child, as the Son of God, the parents obviously knew that, and there must have been times when they were tempted to push Him further and faster into His ministry.

On the surface, it would seem inconceivable to them to think that it would take the Son of God thirty years before He would begin His ministry. Perhaps they would become impatient along the way. In fact, remember how Mary called on her son to solve the wine shortage problem at the marriage at Cana. Jesus' reply almost shocks us as He said, *"Woman, what does your concern have to do with me?"* (John 2:4). Really, that was a very gentle and loving rebuke in which He was saying, as is recorded immediately after those words, *"My hour has not yet come."*

Perhaps there may have been such times when He was given a push, but by and large the Bible makes it clear that they did permit Him to progress naturally, according to God's timetable.

Remember again how, as a 12-year-old boy, Jesus remained behind in Jerusalem in the observance of Passover. When His parents found Him missing and returned to search for Him, they would discover Him in the temple, where He dialogued with the Elders. Do you recall Jesus' response when they expressed their concern? He said to them, *"Why did you seek me? Did you not know that I must be about my Father's business?"* (Luke 2:49). There is no record that they expressed displeasure at His response, indicative that they *were* permitting Him to develop as the Son of God for His assigned ministry.

Now this is not to say that children should not be challenged and stretched; they should be, but don't push, *encourage* natural growth.

At this point, permit me to put in a word for the children. I grow tired of the efforts of the state to push our children, seemingly unwilling to permit them the leisure to enjoy life as they develop naturally. They endeavor to take their relaxed family experience of childhood away through such efforts as "Head Start." Permit the parents to give their children a "head start" if they so desire! Parents are well able to teach their children the ABCs, how to count, and some basic exercises in comprehension. Don't rob the children by permitting the parents to "pass the buck" to a governmental program. Then there is "year around" school, robbing the children of their summer leisure, summer pursuits in which they play, work, and learn to earn, enjoying longer hours in the family. Those summers are just as important to children as a semester of school, perhaps even more valuable if the truth be known.

Parents should tell the state, through its school system, to butt out and permit us to simply encourage natural growth in our children.

Step Three

A third step in the biblical way of setting children free is to *develop responsibility* in them.

The world's children's liberation movement would remove all responsibility, this effort being seen in the permissive attitude prevailing today, as seen in children running to and fro unsupervised on the streets, driving luxury automobiles, indulged at almost every whim, every desire.

Now it is true that parents, not the state, are to provide for their needs, as the Bible tells us in Paul's first letter to Timothy, chapter 5 and verse 8, *"But if anyone does not provide for his own, and especially for those of his household, he has denied the faith and is worse than an unbeliever."* Does this mean that parents are to deliver everything on "a silver platter" to their children, not teaching them to earn their way? The answer is obviously "no."

We read in Lamentations, chapter 3, verse 27, *"It is good for a man to bear the yoke in his youth."*

The imagery here is of the oxen yoked and pulling the load. The lesson depicted emphasizes that children should assist, should be enabled, should be permitted, and expected to help carry the load, even in their youth. Children need to learn to work, need work to do, being taught to take care of their own needs.

They should be given responsibility, opportunities in the decision-making process, even being permitted to fail at times, thereby learning from their failures.

My two boys had jobs one summer and overslept one morning because they failed to set the alarm the night before. As they overslept, they were rushing around the next morning, almost missing their ride to work. Actually, I had to give a ride to one of them, but I told them both afterwards, "This is it, no more. You get up and get to work on your own."

Their mother said sleepily the next morning or two as I would be making my way to the office, "better check on the boys to see if they are up." I didn't tell her, but I had determined that I would not check on them in seeing whether they had arisen or not, giving them an opportunity to fail and even lose their jobs if need be, possibly learning responsibility through failure. Children must learn responsibility even if they fail at times. However, parents indulging children often do not require responsible action, with little being required of them at home.

My dad taught me how to work. As long as I can remember that old cotton farm in West Texas, I can recall learning to work and work hard. When cotton-picking time came, as a small preschool lad, I would be expected to take a center row of cotton to pick between my mother and dad. They would be picking cotton from two rows on each side of me, while I was responsible for the row in between. If I fell behind, my dad would encourage me along, even reaching over to help catch me up occasionally.

When it came time to milk the cows, as early as I can remember, I was started with the responsibility of putting out feed. Then I ultimately graduated to the place where

I could milk the easiest cow there was to milk. Then ultimately, gradually, I gained the responsibility of carrying a full load.

On the other hand, my mother, in her mother's love, did a real disservice to me. Before I left home in my early twenties, after a stint of military service in the Second World War, I would go home at night, just throwing my clothes on the floor. My mother would pick them up the next morning and care for them. If I came home late, she could hear me come in, and she would ask, "Glennon, are you hungry?" When I answered "yes," she would get out of bed and feed me, teaching me some poor habits and irresponsibility. However, I must confess that my wife broke those habits early in our marriage!

Nevertheless, I learned responsibility where it counted, in work and the use of my time. What is happening to youth today? Go to school, and one finds kids driving fancy, expensive automobiles with little responsibility, almost always purchased by their parents. Such was the case with a participant at Columbine High, as he drove his BMW.

One may think I was harsh, but I helped my children get their own cars after they got out of high school, when they were able to go to work, pay for them, and pay the expenses for operating them. They were not keeping up with the Jones', and probably felt deprived at times, but they were learning responsibility.

Looking again at the example of Jesus, our attention is drawn to the Gospel of Luke, chapter 2, verse 21, where we are told how He returned home from Jerusalem with His parents, and *"was subject to them."* Although He was the Son of God, He continued in subjection to His parents. He worked as a carpenter in Joseph's carpenter shop, coming to be known as a carpenter. We read in Mark, chapter 6, verse 3, *"Is not this the carpenter, the son of Mary?"* Perhaps it would have been easy for Mary to say, "Joseph, it isn't fitting

that the Son of God work in that dirty old carpenter's shop."
But no, He continued in subjection, even the Son of God
learned responsibility.

Step Four

Another step in preparing to liberate your children the
biblical way is *don't overprotect your children.* As was
observed earlier, children must be permitted to learn through
failure, and even through times of testing. Consider the prod-
igal son in this connection. When he went to his father and
demanded his inheritance, obviously old enough to receive it,
his father probably reasoned with him, and could have ultimately denied his demands. His father could have said, "Son,
you cannot have your inheritance for your own good."

However, it evidently *was* for his own good, the prod-
igal obviously old enough to demand and receive his inheritance. To deny it could have simply driven him to rebellion.
Consequently, the best thing, and the only way he would
truly learn responsibility, was for him to be given those
possessions, permitting him to end up with the pigs, where
he would *"come to himself"* (Luke 15:17), realizing the error
of his ways. Apparently he had to fail to learn the proper
course for his life.

An interesting reference is found in the letter to the
Hebrews, chapter 5, verses 7 and 8. Total understanding
of the words found here is difficult, and yet we are told
concerning the Lord Jesus Christ, *"Who, in the days of His
flesh, when He had offered up prayers and supplications,
with vehement cries and tears to Him who was able to save
Him from death, and was heard because of His godly fear,
though He was a son, yet He learned obedience by the things
which He suffered."*

I don't pretend to be able to explain that statement, but
obviously as we take it at "face value," Jesus did learn obedi-

ence through suffering. He did not suffer as a sinner, as the perfect Son of God, but He did suffer and learned obedience from it in some unexplainable way.

Yet, what do parents more often do in the face of potential difficulties? They are inclined to keep their children under their wings, in order that they may never get hurt. When the children are facing problems, the temptation is always to draw them in and draw them out of failure, not permitting them to work their way through their difficulties and learn from them. In doing this, parents deny them the learning process, denying them the opportunity to learn the lesson the only way it may ever be learned.

Step Five

A fifth step in preparing children to leave the nest is *a strong husband/wife relationship that is not dependent on the children.*

The outline for the proper husband/wife relationship is found in Paul's letter to the Ephesians, chapter five, verses 22 through 33. Here the wife is instructed to be *"in submission"* to her husband; the husband is told to love his wife as Christ loved the church and died for it. That relationship is to be as strong as the relationship between Christ and the church.

Yet, all too often parents place the relationship with their children above that one with their partner. Consequently, they try to hold on to the children, not willing to let them go. Many times, because of this over emphasis on the children at the expense of their own relationship, once the nest is emptied, the parents are unable to find a fulfilling relationship. Recently a mother, speaking of her son's unhappiness, told of how when her son's child left home, her son's wife proclaimed life to be over, nothing more for which to live. Although not verbalized so clearly and forcefully, that attitude prevails all too often in varying degrees, leading to varying measures of unhappiness, and even in divorce in the case just referenced.

Husbands and wives need time together so as to build their relationship in preparing to liberate their children. If they fail, disaster will result, that is, if they depend on their children to bring fulfillment and depend on them to hold their marriage together. Wayne Dehoney, speaking of marriage said, *"Marriage is like driving a car. You must keep your hands on the wheel throughout the journey, not just at the outset."*

We find that in this final step in freeing children, during the empty nest period is where so many marriages fail because of an inordinate dependence upon children, while at the same time neglecting 'their' own relationship.

Single parents are particularly vulnerable at these times, and the dangers are multiplied for them, as they are inclined toward developing an unfair dependency on the children, endeavoring to use them in replacing the missing partner.

Parents, married or single, must exercise special care so as not to fall into the trap being discussed. In doing so, they place such a responsibility on their children that they cannot properly liberate them when the time to do so arrives.

Here are some steps, some common sense Scriptural steps to take in preparing for responsible children's liberation - the biblical way.

Child Liberation is a Process

Liberating children is a *process*, and that process should begin with the conception of the child, continuing through infancy, through the varying school ages, continuing until the child is launched, or the arrow is turned loose to hit the target, and they are set free.

Not a Sudden Event

Liberation is not a sudden event. Hear these words recorded in Psalm 144, verse 12, *"That our sons may be as plants grown up in their youth, That our daughters may be as pillars, sculptured in palace style."*

The inspired Psalmist is emphasizing that our focus should be on the finished product. When they come to that point of maturity, then they can release their sons and daughters with confidence. And so again, in this connection, our goal will always be toward balance, as once again demonstrated in the life of our Savior.

That wonderful balance is revealed in the observation recorded in the gospel according to Luke, chapter 2, verse 52, *"And Jesus increased in wisdom and stature, and in favor with God and men."*

He grew with balance, not only physically but also spiritually; He grew in favor with both God and men.

The word *"increased"* reveals that growth is a process, one that is gradual by nature. For a fuller understanding of this process, our attention should be turned to Paul's second letter to Timothy, following first the words found in chapter 3, verses 13 through 16. We read these words in verse thirteen, *"But evil men and impostors will grow worse and worse, deceiving and being deceived."*

The great Apostle was telling Timothy that times are bad and will get worse, going from bad to worse, with deception becoming more a way of life—a description which sounds like the twenty-first century!

As Paul cautions Timothy against falling into the snares of the deceivers, he reveals certain steps that have been taken in Timothy's life that will provide his defenses.

An examination of these steps should equip us to prepare the children for a similar set of defenses.

Knowledge

First, we find that "knowledge" of the truth had been imparted to Timothy, *"And that from childhood you have known the Holy Scriptures."*

Timothy had knowledge. Where did he get it? The answer is found in chapter 1, verse 5 as Paul instructs Timothy, *"Call to remembrance the genuine faith that is in you, which dwelt first in your grandmother Lois and in your mother Eunice, and I am persuaded is in you also."*

Timothy got his knowledge from his mother and grandmother, Eunice and Lois. The Bible tells us that Timothy's father was a Greek, probably meaning that he was not a believer. Consequently, his instruction in God's Word was passed from his grandmother through his mother.

The first step in the process of liberation is the giving of eternal truth by parents.

Learning

The second step in the liberation process is *learning.* Consider the learning that took place in young Timothy's life, as we read from verse 14, *"But you must continue in the things which you have learned."*

Here is the *assimilation* of that knowledge which the parents have given, revealing the application of knowledge to the child!

Convictions

Knowledge learned results in *convictions* regarding the truth and its application to life. Here are convictions by which the child can live in confidence. Conviction follows learning as revealed in verse fourteen, *"But you must continue in the things which you have learned and been assured of."*

The word *assurance* mans to have conviction, and children really begin to grow when they have values of their own, on which they can build their own lives, no longer being dependent on their parents knowledge, now having those truths they can call their own.

Wisdom

Wisdom is the final step in the growth process. Remember that *wisdom* is the ability to apply supernatural truth or knowledge to the ordinary affairs of life in a practical way. Wisdom is the practical application of knowledge. Thus, the word wisdom as used here refers to Timothy's ability to take the knowledge his grandmother and mother had imparted to him, and then apply it to his own life in every day living. Paul tells Timothy in verse fifteen, *"And that from childhood you have known the Holy Scriptures, which are able to make you wise for salvation through faith which is in Christ Jesus."*

We are told concerning Jesus in Luke, chapter 2, verse 40, *"And the child grew and became strong in spirit, filled with wisdom; and the grace of God was upon him."*

Again in Luke, chapter 2, verse 52, we find that *"Jesus increased in wisdom thus in stature, and in favor with God and men."*

The child's liberation, which includes maturity and responsibility, is not automatic nor a sudden event, but a gradual process, contrasted with the secular humanist concept of liberation as a right of the child, regardless of maturity or responsibility.

The Goal: Maturity

The parent's ultimate goal for their children, at the time of liberation, is *maturity.*

Marks of maturity are to be found in the letter to the Ephesians, chapter 4, verses 11 and 12. As we read there, we will remember how God has placed certain individuals in the church, apostles, prophets, evangelists, and pastor-teachers to perform the tasks of equipping or perfecting the saints for the work of the ministry.

A part of the purpose to be fulfilled by their ministry is found in verse fourteen, where we are told that, *"we should no longer be children." That is, that they grow up and cease being childlike.* A careful study of the remainder of this chapter will reveal certain marks of maturity.

How do you know when your child is mature? How can young people know that they are actually mature, or in the process of maturing? Suppose we briefly review the marks of maturity found here in this chapter of Scripture.

The Marks of Maturity

Stability

The first mark of maturity, seen in the passage before us, is stability, found in the purpose clause which begins with the word "that," in order that, Paul wrote, *"we should no longer be children, tossed to and fro and carried about with every wind of doctrine"* (verse 15).

We see so much instability today, even in the lives of Christians and in churches, people seeking after entertainment, new emotional experiences, running after every new wind of teaching, not growing, not stable. The first mark of maturity is stability.

Truthfulness

The second mark of maturity is *truthfulness,* as our text continues, *"but speaking the truth in love."*

Children often speak the truth, even being brutal as they do so. If you broke your leg, a child might laugh at you. So notice that one is to *"speak the truth in love."* Here is the kind of truth that demonstrates maturity.

For example, my teeth are stained brown, resulting from drinking water heavy in mineral content as a small child. While in the church parking lot one day, talking to a young boy in the community, he said to me, "You need to brush your teeth." That's the way children can be brutally truthful, not thinking about being truthful in love. Well, I very carefully explained to that small boy about the water that made my teeth naturally brown, and that I actually brushed about three or more times a day. As he sat astride his bike he looked at me, skeptically, as though to say, "Yeah, I've tried stories like that myself."

The second mark of maturity is truthfulness expressed in love.

Trust In the Lord

A third mark of maturity is a sound spiritual identity with reliance on the Lord. We read in verse fifteen, *"grow up in all things into Him who is the head—Christ."* We find that the mature lean on Christ, while the immature lean on people.

Unselfishness

A fourth mark of maturity is *unselfishness.* We find in verse sixteen that *"every joint supplies "* his own part of the glue that holds the body together and brings unity. The mature says, "let me share," but the immature child says, "mine, mine," as he gathers all of his possessions together to hoard them.

Self Control

Another mark of maturity is *self control*, as clearly indicated in verses 26-31. *"Be angry and do not sin;" "Give no place to the devil," "Let him who stole, steal no longer, but rather let him labor;" "Let no corrupt word proceed out of your mouth;" "Do not grieve the Holy Spirit of God;"* and finally, *"Let all bitterness, wrath, anger, clamor, and evil speaking be put away from you, with all malice."* Here is the breaking of the individual's bent toward evil.

Christ-Likeness

Finally, we find that the ultimate mark of maturity is *Christ-likeness.*

"And be kind to one another, tenderhearted, forgiving one another, even as God in Christ forgave you."

Here is the list of mature attributes that translate into Christ-likeness—kindness, tenderheartedness, forgiving.

Once the child begins to give evidence of these six marks of maturity, they are ready for liberation the biblical way, not the phony kind of children's liberation preached by the secular humanist.

Summary

Parents are to be reminded that proper liberation does not mean breaking diplomatic relations. When your children are launched, that doesn't mean that they are out of your life, meaning that you no longer *talk* to them and that you are no longer friends.

When parents properly release their children, it should be done in such a way that they can feel free to give counsel, and the "children" will feel free to receive it without being threatened or intimidated. Some of the wisest counsel that I have received since I married came from my dad. He felt free to give it, and I felt perfectly free to receive it and considered the counsel without thinking he was interfering.

We read in Proverbs, chapter 23, verse 22, *"Listen to your father who begot you, and do not despise your mother when she is old."*

My 41-year-old pastor-son called me recently, troubled with a problem and seeking counsel. He felt free to ask, and I felt free to give but not in a meddling, interfering fashion. Relations with the liberated son and daughter should be like that.

Train up a child in this way—develop them for true liberation, the biblical way, and great will be the resulting blessings. But liberation apart from responsibility, as advocated by the secular children's and feminist liberationists, will result in failure for parents and disaster for the children and family.

The results of the kind of training and liberation being advocated are summed up in these words given in relation to Jesus, Luke, chapter 2, verse 40, *"and the grace of God was upon Him."* When parents faithfully discharge their parental responsibility, the grace of God *will be* upon their children.

The kind of results we seek will require great trust in God and much time in prayer. Remember our earlier references to Susanna Wesley. She had given birth to nineteen children. Recall that we said that she gave every one of her nineteen children one hour per week. She spent an hour just for them, just with them—every week!

How many mothers do that with just two or three children? But something I didn't tell you before, when Susanna Wesley's children grew up and left home, she still gave them that same hour every week, but that hour was spent in prayer for them!

Here is true liberation, when you can set them free, turning them over to God.

Notes

1. Richard Farson, Birthrights: A Children's Bill of Rights.

All Scriptures quoted in New King James Version, Thomas Nelson Publishers, unless otherwise noted.

Chapter Fourteen

Bringing the Children to Jesus

The questions asked of Jesus by His disciples intrigue us, as we identify the things in which they were interested. They would ask, just prior to His ascension, *"Lord, will you at this time restore the kingdom to Israel?"* (Acts 1:6). They wanted to know, what will happen to us? What about the future? What does the future hold? Again, they would ask, *"Tell us, when will these things be? And what will be the sign of your coming, and of the end of the age?"* (Matt. 24:3). They desired to know about the future, and so do we.

There were other things that interested them greatly. The disciples plied the Master with questions about who would hold first place with Him. They wanted to know about His miracles, and in response they asked at one point, who then can be saved?

But then, there came those bringing the children to Jesus, resulting in the interruption of a discussion with the Pharisees. This disruption is recorded in the gospel according to Mark, chapter 10, verse 13, *"Then they brought little children to Him, that He might touch them; but the disciples rebuked those who brought them."*

The Pharisees had been querying about the legality of divorce, and while Jesus was in the midst of His answer to these questions, there came those bringing the children. No doubt the disciples were intensely interested in the Master's comments regarding this difficult matter, thus being greatly irritated at the disruption they *"rebuked those who brought the children."*

In the past thirteen chapters we have been considering the dangers that threaten our families, recognizing that the efforts of the extreme feminists in "women's liberation," the efforts of the proponents of "children's liberation," as promoted by the United Nations in their proclamation regarding "The Year of the Child," the efforts of John Dewey and the "progressive education" movement, and the efforts of the secular humanists have been designed to fragment and destroy the traditional family unit—*efforts that thwart parents in bringing their children to Jesus!*

As one reviews chapter titles, it becomes apparent that the problem, as well as its solution, has been thoroughly considered. We have considered the problem and its solution, as it impacts our entire society, as well as the family.

As we begin to conclude this treatise, dealing here with the keystone to the solution, we find that great efforts are still being made in stopping the children from coming to the Savior. Even Christians are often guilty at this very point. Pleas go out for involvement in children's ministries, good news clubs, vacation Bible school, and Sunday school, and multitudes of Christians resist the call with myriads of excuses, demonstrating a lack of interest.

Yet, what was our Savior's response to efforts in resisting the coming of children to Himself? We are told that He was greatly displeased and said to them, *"Let the little children come to me, and do not forbid them; for of such is the Kingdom of God"* (Mark 10:14).

Then the Master expresses Himself more forcefully concerning this matter as we find in Luke's gospel, *"It would be better for him if a millstone were hung around his neck, and be thrown into the sea, than that he should offend one of these little ones"* (Luke 17:2).

Jesus made it crystal clear that we are to be concerned about the children, and about anything that endangers them. *Bringing children to Christ, and seeing that nothing interferes with their coming, is of supreme importance!* Thus, the aim of this concluding chapter is to see and understand our responsibility of bringing the children to Christ, the ultimate solution to every problem considered. Whether single adults, young married couples, families with differing ages of children, or even great-great-grandmothers or grandfathers, *all* have a responsibility regarding the children.

For example, Annabel Boothroyd, a member of the church I pastored for almost three decades, Santa Cruz County Director of Child Evangelism, a grandmother with gray hair, all of her children being out of the nest, and now having grandchildren, she and her husband Howard being retired, one could conclude that all of her obligations had been fulfilled.. If anyone could say that they no longer had a responsibility for ministering to children, Annabel could. Yet, she recognized that one does not graduate from this responsibility, and so she gave her life tirelessly, day in and day out, week in and week out, year in and year out, for years in bringing children to Jesus through child evangelism.

Now looking more closely at the Scripture before us, three different types of people will be viewed.

Those Who Brought the Children

First of all are those who brought the children to Jesus. We are told in Mark, chapter 10, verse 13, *"Then they brought little children to Him."* It is interesting to note that they were *"little children,"* or as the Authorized Version translates *"young* children," although we are to bring older children and even adults, the emphasis here is on young or little children.

Remember that Jesus had just returned from Galilee to the coast of Judea, there where He was thronged about with crowds. As was His custom, He taught them, and true to form, the Pharisees came again, endeavoring to trap the Savior, asking Him about the legality of divorce. In His response, the Savior strongly declares the sanctity of marriage, saying, *"what God has joined together, let man not separate."*

It was in such a situation that there were those who broke through the crowd, ignoring the resistance of the disciples, and brought the children to the Master's side. Some have suggested that they must have been the mothers of the children. That probably is true, but think about what caused them to come, and what caused them to think they would be received favorably.

Divorce was a thing of relative ease, in which a husband could put away his wife for virtually any reason. Remember the question the Pharisees had asked, *"Is it lawful for a man to divorce his wife?"* Matthew adds to that question in his account, *"Is it lawful for a man to divorce his wife for every cause?"*

Consequently, at that time in history, the family was constantly in jeopardy, as husbands divorced their wives frivolously for "every cause." Here were mothers and wives, who would be attentive to the teaching of the Savior as He declared the security and sanctity of marriage. They would conclude that, anyone who gave such support to the family, would have a genuine interest in children, and that His love and acceptance of them would not be questioned.

The repeated emphasis in this treatise is that, the first responsibility of parents is to teach children God's Word, thus introducing them to a personal relationship with the

Savior, bringing them to Jesus. That same responsibility belongs to the Church, to everyone.

Yet, why did these individuals, mothers or not, desire that the children come to Christ? We read again, *"they brought little children,"* but why did they bring them? The reason is evident as the account continues, *"that He might touch them,"* and Matthew adds the words, *"and pray."* They brought the children to Jesus in order that He might touch them and pray for them. They desired the Lord's blessings and prayers, the ministry of the Master in their lives. In other words, let the Lord of the home be the Lord and Savior of the children.

But why the desire for such a touch? That touch would represent His blessings, with a deeper meaning being captured in a song often sung,

"Shackled by a heavy burden,
'neath a load guilt and shame,
Then the hand of Jesus touched me,
And now I am no longer the same,
He touched me."

Here was the touch that these people wanted for the children. The first responsibility of parents and others is to bring the children to Jesus for His touch, an effort that will be costly, that will cost us time, cost us inconvenience and effort, and maybe, as in this case, ridicule, but our responsibility is to bring the children to Jesus, the only source of cleansing and wholeness for them.

The People Who Barred the Way

Next, we see the disciples who barred the children's way. The disciples were just human and selfish enough to resent the interruption of the interesting exchange taking place between Jesus and the Pharisees. They had repeatedly seen the Pharisees come in an effort to trap the Savior, and again and again had listened to His response as He had, without exception, emerged victorious. Furthermore, they would have been intrigued by the discussion related to divorce and the implications for potential remarriage. Consequently they would resent the interruption of those who brought the children.

People today are resentful when they do not hear what they desire to hear, perhaps even from the pulpit. One may understand the disciples interest, but there can be no excuse as we read, *"the disciples rebuked those who brought them."* "Don't bother the master," they would say, "He is busy in an important discussion. How dare you interrupt, you are not even on the schedule or order of service!"

Two words characterize their attitude.

Irritation

First, they were *irritated*. They were so angry that anyone could be so presumptuous as to think children were important enough to interrupt a theological discussion. Get those kids out of here! Can't you see that we are busy?

Insensitive

Next, they were *insensitive* to the spiritual needs of the children and their importance. They could not imagine a King who had come to establish a kingdom, who would have time for mere children who could not vote, who could not fight in an army, and furthermore had no money with which to pay taxes.

Luis Palau, world-renowned Latin American evangelist, wrote about an evangelistic crusade being conducted in La Paz, Bolivia. Luis wrote in his letter about how he had been looking forward with keen anticipation to a luncheon with the president of the country, providing an opportunity to talk with him personally. Luis has introduced a number of officials and leaders to Christ, and on this day, he was looking forward to that appointment.

However, a news conference was scheduled for mid-morning, preceding the presidential appointment. The newsmen had come to his hotel room, and since they were Marxist oriented, before long they were involved in a rather lively discussion. In the midst of this discussion, a knock came on the door, and a team member entered bringing a little 11-year-old girl with him, the daughter of the elevator operator of the hotel where evangelist Palau was staying.

The little girl had been watching Luis every night on television, and now she wanted to talk to him. Luis said that he was really upset with the team member, thinking, what in the world is he doing, bringing a little girl into the middle of a press meeting? Consequently he reached down, plucked up a book, and upon signing it, he handed it to her, saying, "the Lord bless you sweetheart." As he began ushering her toward the door, she stopped and protested, "But, Mr. Palau, I wanted to receive Christ into my heart."

Even this great evangelist had resented that interruption, demonstrating that things have not changed since the day the disciples endeavored to turn the children away. But Luis was sensitive to the leading of the Holy Spirit, and rebuked by his own attitude, he excused himself, sat down, and presented the Gospel to the little 11-year-old, leading her to Christ.

Yet it is true that we rebuke and reject the children in many ways. We don't want to bother with them, and so we shuffle them off and out of our way. The call goes out for workers for children's Bible clubs, vacation Bible school, or teachers for children's Sunday school classes, and the call is met with negative responses. "I don't have time," some say. Others refuse to respond, saying, "I'm not qualified." An answer often heard from the older folks, "Get the young mothers to do it," as though they have graduated from the responsibility. Although one would not hear it verbalized, others may shrug off the need, saying to themselves, "After all, they're only a bunch of kids."

During my twenty-eight year ministry in one church, we started bus ministries twice. That ministry would result in an influx of unsupervised, undisciplined children. They would scratch the pews, track dirt on the carpet, make noise, and cause all kinds of disruptions in the worship services. One may be sure that there were many who were not sorry to see those ministries end, people who were ready to "get rid of those kids." We'll not be harsh, will we, for after all the disciples were guilty of the same.

The One Who Blessed

Next, after the abortive effort of the disciples, *Jesus blessed* the children. When He observed the actions of His followers, *"He was greatly displeased."* He was displeased when His dearest friends rejected and neglected these little ones, and we may be sure that He is displeased when we neglect them too. If such rejection caused His displeasure two thousand years ago, we may be sure that His response is the same today, for the Bible tells us that, *"He is the same yesterday, today and forever"* (Heb. 13:8).

An old pastor in Scotland, so the story goes, persisted in denying church membership to children. One day an old elder in his church invited the pastor to his farm, and while he was there, the elder, who was also a shepherd, began putting the sheep into the sheepfold. The elder did an unusual thing as he would only permit the older sheep to enter the fold, while taking his shepherd's crook and cruelly thrusting and turning the lambs away, not permitting them to enter.

The pastor watched for awhile, and then he said to the elder, "How cruel. Why are you not permitting the lambs to enter the protection of the sheepfold? They need the shelter more than the older sheep." The old shepherd, making his point, said solemnly, "I'm just doing what you do to the lambs of the church."

Are you driving the children away, or are you leading them to the Savior? Oh no, the protest may be, I may not be bringing them to Jesus, but I'm not driving them away. But listen to these words of the Savior, and feel His displeasure, *"He who is not with me is against me, and he who does not gather with me scatters abroad"* (Matt. 12:30).

First, the Master was displeased with the action of the disciples. Next He said, *"Permit the little children to come to me, and do not forbid them."* He was concerned for the little ones, and desires that we are also. But the disciples, at that point in time, were more concerned in throwing off the yoke of Rome, but the Savior was more concerned about blessing the children.

Summary

On one occasion there was a great celebration on behalf of Queen Victoria, Queen of England. The mayor of the city received a message from the queen after the celebration. Thinking that the message might contain some compliment, he opened it only to find much different words than those anticipated. The message read, "The queen wants to know whether all of the children got home safely!" That's the concern of the King of Kings. He is concerned for the children, asking His servants to look after the welfare of the little people. His servants may be assured that He will receive them when they do. We read in Mark, chapter 10, verse 16, *"And He took them up in His arms, laid His hands on them, and blessed them."*

A wonderful story is told about the great Italian general and liberator, Garibaldi. One day Garibaldi met a shepherd with a sad countenance, and asked if there was anything he could do to help. The shepherd answered, "Nothing. I fear, sir, I've lost one of my lambs." Garibaldi turned to his staff to announce to them that he was going out to search for the lamb, with a number of them going along.

After a period of time, meeting with failure, those staff members returned to their barracks. The next morning when the general's servant looked for Garibaldi, not only was the general not in bed, but the servant discovered that the bed was undisturbed from the previous night.

The servant quickly gathered men together to search for the general, and when they found him, Garibaldi was lying asleep by the side of the road where the little lamb was cuddled nearby, covered by the general's cape.

Here is the lesson Jesus' disciples needed to learn in their self-centeredness and hardness of heart, and the lesson we need to learn—Jesus cares for the little lambs, the little children.

The prophet Isaiah, foreseeing this concern, prophesied, *"He will feed His flock like a shepherd; He will gather the lambs with His arm, And carry them in His bosom, and gently lead those who are with young"* (Isaiah 40:11).

We find not just a Christian alternative, but the only solution to the threat to our children, to our families, to our land.

Prayer: Father, we see the tremendous responsibility that belongs to us, and our minds and hearts are sobered to realize its not enough just to point our fingers at the world and its excesses, and blame the humanists and others for all of the failures.

And our Father, we are impressed anew that the solution and responsibility for the solution rests completely with us.

Father God, help us to cease handing over the responsibility for the teaching of our children to others and cause each one of us to assume that responsibility in a new and more determined way than ever.

Again, dear Father, impress upon us this day the tremendous obligation that is ours. Impress upon us again that we have the only real and lasting solution. And, oh Father, cause us to reorder our priorities so that we might be involved, no matter what our station in life, no matter what our age might be, in bringing the "little ones" to the Savior.

Printed in the United States
48755LVS00005BA/148-510

9 781597 818339